Faith in a Global Economy

Rob van Drimmelen
Preface by D. Preman Niles

Faith in a Global Economy

A Primer for Christians

Risk
BOOK SERIES

WCC Publications, Geneva

Cover design: Edwin Hassink

IBSN 2-8254-1254-6

© 1998 WCC Publications, World Council of Churches,
150 route de Ferney, 1211 Geneva 2, Switzerland

No. 81 in the Risk Book Series

Printed in Switzerland

To
Philip A. Potter

Table of Contents

Preface

"Give to Caesar the things that are Caesar's, and to God the things that are God's" (Mark 12:17). "You cannot serve both God and Mammon" (Luke 16:13b). Placing these sayings of Jesus side by side, we might easily conclude that while it is possible to distinguish between the legitimate claims of the political realm and of faith, no such choice is possible when it comes to the realms of economics and of faith. Here the choice seems absolute. One cannot serve both God and Mammon.

So, perplexed by the complexities of the world economic system and angry about the suffering of the poor and the plight of a devastated environment, we slip easily into the rhetoric of "either-or" – either condemn or commend. We fall into the trap of seeking simple answers to complex questions. Such an approach is not possible today. Nor was it possible in the time of Jesus. For even the first saying quoted above, which assumes that it is possible to distinguish between legitimate allegiance to political authority and one's allegiance to God, comes in the context of paying taxes. It has as much to do with economics as with politics. The second saying of Jesus cited seems to imply that allegiances to God and Mammon are mutually exclusive. Yet, in the preceding verses, Jesus commends a dishonest manager for the way in which he uses "the Mammon of unrighteousness" or "dishonest wealth", holding this up as an example of how "the children of this age are more shrewd in dealing with their own generation than are the children of light" (Luke 16:8-9).

These sayings of Jesus illustrate the complicated relationships that exist between the realms of politics, economics and faith, and the problems they pose for social ethics. In this book, Rob van Drimmelen brings to bear on this complicated area his knowledge and experience as a banker, economist and ecumenical worker. With clarity, he unravels for readers the complex economic relations that exist today, lays bare the messianic claims of the world market and debunks the religious language of economic pretensions. With equal skill he shows the connections between economics, politics and the Christian faith, the ways in which economic considerations are becoming determinative for political thinking and how these impact on ethics. The book is both erudite and access-ible. It also ends with practical examples of "going against the tide". Having read these chapters, I am glad I nagged Rob to write this book.

It is appropriate that this book is dedicated to Philip Potter. Especially since his retirement as general secretary of the World Council of Churches in 1984, Philip has devoted much time and study to the relationship between economics and faith. When he was WCC general secretary, he involved the ecumenical movement in tackling issues of justice, peace and the integrity of creation and their implications for the mission of the church. Often criticized by those within and vilified by those without, he remained a model of costly commitment for us who worked with him and followed him.

D. Preman Niles
General Secretary
Council for World Mission, London

Introduction

In the main building of the Free University in Amsterdam, the offices of the faculty of economics are on the bottom floors whereas the faculty of theology is at the top, many stories above. The location of these two faculties reflects the way many people perceive the relationship between economy and theology: economics has both feet on the ground, theology has its head in the clouds and there is a great distance between the two.

Nevertheless, over the last 15 years or so, more and more people have begun to reflect about the relationships between Christian faith and economic life. A wide spectrum of churches and Christian organizations have made studies and issued statements, declarations and pastoral messages on economic issues. While some might argue that these topics are better left to economists and politicians, the fact is that Christian faith cannot make a separation between spiritual and material life. Economics is about people's daily life: procuring food, shelter and clothes, performing meaningful work. God became incarnate in Christ to share the human condition with us. The Lord's Prayer speaks about daily bread and forgiving debts – the most pressing issues for those who heard Jesus in the first century, as they are for millions of people in the world today. It would be as wrong to separate this petition for our daily bread from the meaning of the eucharistic bread as to interpret the forgiving of debts only in a spiritual way. If people are starving, it is as much a religious as an economic problem.

God's economy

The word "economy" comes from the Greek words *oikos*, meaning house or household, and *nomos*, meaning law or rules. Economics, therefore, literally refers to applying "household rules" – and in this sense economics is as old as humanity, because people have always used household rules. But as the Orthodox Christian tradition reminds us, "economy" has a special use in Christian theology to point to the incarnation of God in Christ. The coming of Jesus was God's special way of "home management" in order to save the world. The central theme of the divine economy is *kenosis*, God's self-emptying through the death of Jesus on the cross.

In Christ's offering, the whole created order was offered to God; and the Orthodox tradition understands every eucharistic celebration as a participation in this self-offering of Christ. In the eucharist – which means "thanksgiving" – we offer bread and wine, the fruits of human labour and the symbols of the whole material creation, to the eternal God through Christ. In return we receive the body and blood of Christ.[1] The eucharist exemplifies the cooperation between God and us for our sustenance and the transformation of the world. We find our purpose in this invitation to be co-workers with God. This link between "daily bread" and the bread of the eucharist illustrates the inseparable connection between the divine economy and the secular economy, the spiritual and the material.

Oikonomia, koinonia and oikoumene

Like many households, God's household is structured around a table, the table of bread and wine. This indicates that God's economy aims at establishing community or *koinonia*, of which the Holy Trinity is the supreme model. When Christ quoted Deuteronomy 8:3 to insist that "one does not live by bread alone", he was reaffirming the link between the spiritual duty of the community and the socio-economic needs of the poor. This emphasis on building up community through economic policies and systems contrasts sharply with political and economic systems based on ruthless competition in the pursuit of individual gain.

Of course, there are many groups which like to think of themselves as communities – including some business corporations. The question is whether they are inclusive or exclusive communities. Who is included in the "community" of a company if it defines its nature and raison d'être vis-à-vis other companies? How much of a real community is the European Union (formerly called the European *Community*), given the growing gap between rich and poor within its own borders? Are these communities based on the principles of organized care – or organized selfishness?

The Old Testament is full of rules given by God for the management of the household, the economy, of the people of Israel. The prescriptions for the sabbath, the sabbath year and the jubilee year are probably among the best known. These covenantal obligations aimed at safeguarding the creation and protecting the most vulnerable people in society: the poor, widows and orphans, lepers, strangers and sojourners.

Some of the household rules given by God were rather radical, apparently because free market forces alone do not create economic justice. The Bible does not refer to any sacred law of supply and demand. Yahweh asks for justice. Just institutions and laws, including some which "intervene" in the "market", were to be set up to protect the poor, the vulnerable and creation as a whole.

This is not to say that we should try to re-establish the prescriptions of the Hebrew Scriptures for economic life today. The poor in Sudan would not benefit if French farmers were to refrain from mowing the edges of their fields (Deut. 24:19). Instead, we should try to follow the biblical mandate to set up economically and environmentally just mechanisms and institutions. We must ask who are the people *today* who "join house to house and add field to field" (Isa. 5:8) at the expense of economic justice. Who are the poor, the lepers, the widows, the orphans, the strangers of our time? How can we be like the caring and sharing community described in Acts 2 and 4?

This book is an attempt to give an overview of and introduction to some of the main economic issues of today, drawing on the discussion of these within the ecumenical movement. The focus is contemporary; historical surveys of the ecumenical debate about economic issues can be found elsewhere.[2] But even an introduction cannot be neutral; thus it is only fair to say from the outset that what follows reflects the biases of one who is inspired by the ecumenical vision of justice, peace and respect for God's creation. It must immediately be added that differences of opinion also exist among those who share this vision. There is a lively ecumenical debate about social issues, but there is no such thing as a single ecumenical social teaching. I hope this book will contribute to that ecumenical debate about how we can live out our Christian faith in a global economy.

I close this introduction with some expressions of gratitude. One is to D. Preman Niles, general secretary of the Council for World Mission. Without his persistent encouragement I would not have begun, let alone complete this project. Richard D.N. Dickinson and Bob Goudzwaard read the draft meticulously and I am grateful to them for their comments, as well as to Marlin VanElderen for his editorial work on the book.

Most of all I should like to thank Philip Potter, to whom I have dedicated this book. Since he retired as general secretary of the World Council of Churches in 1984, he has devoted much of his time to studying economics and exploring the interactions between Christian faith and the world economy today. Over the years, his sharp theological and political insights have been a tremendous source of inspiration for me. Through Philip, I am also expressing my gratitude to the ecumenical movement as a whole. Participation in this movement has profoundly influenced my life.

Brussels, June 1998   ROB VAN DRIMMELEN

NOTE

[1] See K.M. George, "Towards a Eucharistic Ecology", in G. Limouris, ed., *Justice, Peace and the Integrity of Creation: Insights from Orthodoxy*, Geneva, WCC, 1990.
[2] See for example Aart van den Berg, *Churches Speak out on Economic Issues: A Survey of Several Statements*, Geneva, WCC, 1990; Robert McAfee Brown and Sydney Thomson Brown, eds, *A Cry for Justice: The Churches and Synagogues Speak*, New York, Paulist Press, 1989; Rob van Drimmelen, "*Homo Oikonomicus* and *Homo Economicus*: Christian Reflection and Action on Economics in the Twentieth Century", *Transformation*, Vol. 4, nos 3-4, June-Sept./Oct.-Dec. 1987; Mark Ellingsen, *The Cutting Edge: How Churches Speak on Social Issues*, Geneva, WCC, 1993.

1. Economics as a Science

If economic systems, as we said in the introduction, are as old as humanity, economics as a science is a relatively new phenomenon. Adam Smith (1723-1790), commonly regarded as the founder of economic science, was a teacher of moral philosophy. Economics, in other words, was originally seen as a normative theory about the production and the distribution of the means to live, clearly related to ethics, history and political science. Adam Smith did not advocate maximizing the "wealth of nations" (to use the title of his famous book) as an abstract goal without regard to distribution; he believed no nation could be strong or happy if most of its people lived in poverty and misery.

Like other sciences, economics became, over the course of time, more and more independent and autonomous. Although such influential economists as Karl Marx and John Maynard Keynes never made a divorce between economics and politics, an important school of thought arose which saw the economy as belonging to a separate sphere of life, dominated by its own independent laws. The laws of supply and demand were regarded as autonomous, neutral and untouchable – like the law of gravity. If these laws were left alone, the pursuit of individual gain would lead, through the invisible hand of the free market mechanism, to the benefit of all. The market became impersonal and anonymous, and the human being was reduced to an individual who carefully calculates his or her benefits and acts accordingly.

The key word here is "individual" because it points to a basic assumption of this emerging science: that of the "rational, utility-maximizing individual". Many mainstream economists take it for granted that rational utility-maximization is a natural attribute deeply ingrained in human nature. Acquisitive behaviour is thus legitimized as a social norm. Moreover, individuals are assumed to behave rationally and to have available perfect knowledge of all the relevant information necessary to make the decisions which would maximize their gain.

Another important basic assumption is that the needs of individuals are unlimited. Scarcity is therefore taken as a given and is not as such studied in mainstream economic theories. No differentiation is made among the needs of individuals, which are expressed in the market through purchasing power; all are treated equally, basic needs or luxury goods and services alike. This explains why mainstream economic theory has long given so little attention to the growing scarcity of "non-monetary goods" like clean water and clean air. The idea that there is "enough for everyone's needs but not enough for everyone's greed" does not say much to such economists, because they do not – and do not wish to – make a distinction between need and greed, since that would undermine the claim that economic science is and ought to be neutral.

Is economics neutral?

But is economics indeed a neutral science with universally valid and applicable laws? Let us approach this question by looking at economics – specifically the three production factors which economists usually identify: labour, capital and land – from the point of view of culture.

Culture affects a range of questions about *labour*: whether work on Sundays is acceptable or not, how slave labour and child labour are seen, how work is divided between women and men, what type of work is remunerated or not (housekeeping and child-rearing vs. school-teaching, for example).

Although the logic of amassing *capital* dominates many societies, it is not in fact universal, nor has it existed throughout history. There have been and are cultures and societies in which people produce or collect only for their immediate needs. There are even cultures in which people compete in giving away instead of accumulating. Recall the portrait of the early Christian community in Acts 2 and 4.[1]

The use of *land* is also heavily influenced by culture. The respect for land and nature which characterizes most indigenous cultures contrasts sharply with the disrespect for creation prevailing in industrial societies. Some indigenous people pray before cutting down a tree, in effect apologizing for their need of the wood or the land on which it was growing. Some parcels of land may be sacred and should not be touched, because ancestors are buried there.

Ownership of these production factors is also seen differently from culture to culture. Private property is valued highly in Northern-type societies, whereas collective use of production factors characterizes many indigenous societies – though it was previously found elsewhere as well (the "commons" in Britain, for example). Likewise, consumption patterns differ according to the cultural context: something judged a need in one culture may be seen as greed or waste in another setting.

One reason why there are different economic systems is that the organization of the economy – who produces what, how, where, when and for whom – is built on history and culture. A system that works in one place may not work in another setting with a different cultural, historical and political background.

It would seem, therefore, that economic "laws" are not in fact neutral or universally valid and applicable. There is a tremendous cultural arrogance behind the idea that Northern-type economic systems and policies are superior to other "primitive" and "inefficient" systems in which prices are based on "irrational" motives – and should thus be transplanted to other cultural settings. Undeniably the logic of Northern-type economic systems, with its concept of efficiency and view of human beings as utility-maximizing individuals, has brought many material blessings, but there are also serious shortcomings. Rather than imposing this system and its logic wholesale on other cultures, it would be better to acknowledge that other cultures also have things to teach – and that by learning from these insights a better understanding of one's own culture is possible.

The importance of culture has been emphasized in recent ecumenical mission discussions. Just as the gospel of Jesus Christ must become incarnate in every culture, and more attention should be given to "contextual theology" and the "inculturation of the gospel", it would be interesting to

extend this discussion to consider what "contextual economy" and the "inculturation of economics" might mean.

Economics always involves value judgments. The economy is not an independent sphere of life governed by neutral
universal laws. Making claims like "the economy demands
such-and-such measures" tends to hide the fact that behind
this "demand" lie choices made by some person or group of
persons on the basis of their values. In this sense, economics
must be demystified. What Adam Smith called the "invisible
hand" which distributes "the necessities of life" has to be
made visible. Power relationships in economic life, the
underlying value judgments and the "hierarchy of values" on
the basis of which critical actors make their choices must be
uncovered.

Quasi-religious elements

Indeed, economics is sometimes presented in quasi-religious terms. This is most evident in advertising campaigns
that appeal to the religious sub-consciousness of potential
buyers. Coca-Cola has promoted its products with texts like:
"Give me your tired ones, your thirsty ones..., those who are
exhausted" and "I was thirsty and I was refreshed". The
opening words of the eucharist appeared on a large Pepsi-
Cola billboard in the Philippines: "Peace be with you". In
fact, Pepsi Cola and other soft drink producers have brought
anything but peace to the Philippines: their decision to
replace cane sugar with other sweeteners in their drinks was
a serious blow to agricultural income on the island of
Negros.

Quasi-religious language for economic discourse can
also be found in articles and editorials. An editorial com-
ment in *The Economist* on the European Bank for Reconstruction and Development (ERBD), formed to lend to countries in Eastern Europe after the Berlin Wall had fallen, said
that the region's "weakened economies must accept the
harsh discipline of free markets. Capitalism will make them
prosperous eventually; before that, it will idle half their
industries and make redundant up to two-thirds of their

workforce." Sacrifice is necessary. Before salvation can be enjoyed, one must go through the wilderness: "The European Bank wants to guide Eastern Europe's economies through this wilderness, dispensing manna when they falter." A bank which takes on the role of Yahweh. The mission of the ERBD is noble; and *The Economist* described its first president, Jacques Attali, as the prophet of free markets in Eastern Europe. His task was not easy and it might take a while before we see the fruits of sacrifice, but "it may comfort Mr Attali to recall that Moses only glimpsed the promised land".[2]

Such secularized eschatology in advertisements and leading newspapers may seem amusing, but it is more serious when quasi-religious elements are discovered in the writings of Nobel Prize-winning economists and other well-known authors. In a book about the corporate world, Roman Catholic ethicist Michael Novak applies texts from Isaiah 53 "to the modern corporation, a much-despised incarnation of God's presence in this world". Novak goes on to mention seven "gifts of grace" given to us by the corporation, concluding: "Its creativity mirrors God's... The corporation also mirrors God's presence through its freedom, by which I mean its independence from the state."[3]

Corporations like the suffering Christ, offering grace to the world, while twisting Jesus' words in their advertising. Sacralized market forces. Redemption through consumption. Obviously, some people have faith in the world economy, but is it a biblical faith to see corporations as an "incarnation of God's presence in this world"? Some would be more inclined to call this idolatry, the worship of false gods.

It is only by God's grace, not the grace offered by corporations, that we will be able to keep faith in a global economy. To keep faith and to act in faith require being informed about what happens in the world. A familiar ecumenical saying speaks of the Christian living in the world with "the Bible in the one hand and the newspaper in the other". It is to what we can read in the newspapers that we turn in the next chapters.

6

NOTES

[1] Marshall Sahlins, who has written on "economic anthropology", quotes the words of a Bushman in the Kalahari desert: "The worst thing is not giving presents. If people do not like each other, but one gives a gift and the other must accept, this brings peace between them. We give what we have. That is the way we live together"; *Stone Age Economics*, London, Tavistock Publications, 1984, p.182.

[2] *The Economist*, 13 Apr. 1991.

[3] Michael Novak and John W. Cooper, *The Corporation: A Theological Inquiry*, Washington, American Enterprise Institute, 1981.

2. The Global Economy

For centuries, economic systems, the "households" to which people applied certain rules for organization, were basically local and national. This has changed dramatically during the 20th century, and especially during the last 50 years or so. Almost everything that is now local is at the same time global – and vice versa. Production processes, investments, trade in goods and services are being more and more integrated into one global market. Lower transportation and communication costs, as well as the reduction of import tariffs, quotas and foreign exchange controls have contributed to the emergence of a single global market for capital, goods and services. An automobile, for example, is hardly a national product any more. Its different parts are produced in many different countries. Rather than "Made in Japan" or "Made in the USA", it would be more appropriate to label certain cars "Made in the World". Credit cards are a typical example of the globalization of services. Some can be used for payments in almost every corner of the world; and in many countries it is more and more difficult to book a hotel room without a credit card. It seems as if a credit card is becoming a more important identification document than a passport.

Globalization

Globalization is one of the most important and, it seems, widely-discussed processes taking place in the world today. Judging by the variety of meanings attributed to it, the word "globalization" apparently means all things to all persons. Often it is blamed for nearly every unwelcome development in the economy or even society as a whole – for example, by governments and international institutions seeking to disavow their own responsibility for it. Such statements are often accompanied by the observation that globalization cannot be stopped and is here to stay; those who oppose it are like the candlemakers who tried to ban the electric light bulb in the 19th century.[1]

Usually, globalization refers to the process of growing and intensifying interaction of all levels of society in world trade, foreign investment and capital markets. It is abetted by technological advances in transport and communications, and by a rapid liberalization and deregulation of trade and capital flows, both nationally and internationally, leading to one global market.

International contacts and exchange are of course nothing new. Migration flows took place in the ancient world. International trading companies existed in the time of the Phoenicians. The Crusades brought different cultures in (violent) contact with each other. European colonization (often accompanied by missionary enterprises) started at the end of the 15th century. Present-day globalization differs from these earlier processes both in nature (its emphasis on liberalization and deregulation) and in scope and intensity. But like colonialism, globalization benefits the powerful economic interests most.

The difference between globalization and internationalism can perhaps be summed up in the observation that almost everybody in the world recognizes the logo of Coca-Cola and the "golden arches" of McDonalds, but very few people would be able to tell you the colour of the flag of the United Nations, let alone the symbol of the ecumenical movement. Globalization focuses on economic processes while internationalism aims at political cooperation. It can be argued that the roots of internationalism lay in the "one world" philosophy which emerged during the period of the Enlightenment in Europe and came to expression in the *Communist Manifesto*, the founding of the League of Nations and, later, the United Nations. It also played a role in the rise of the ecumenical movement and its quest for the unity of the church and the unity of humankind.

Today's globalizers basically accept world economic developments as inevitable, while internationalists want to shape and influence these developments through political intervention. Globalizers applaud the absorption of all countries and systems into one, whereas internationalists speak of other forms of integration and pay special attention to the poor and the marginalized. While internationalism has always aimed at improving relationships between nations, the present process of globalization undermines the very concept of the nation-state. Internationalism is based on the conviction that citizens should be able to influence government policies; globalization erodes national sovereignty and can in the end threaten democracy and people's participation.

The end of the cold war gave a tremendous impetus to globalization. In the ideological competition of the cold war, superpowers had formed worldwide alliances for political and economic power. The Marshall Plan was an early example; later, development assistance policies aimed at a similar goal. Aid went to those who agreed to stay out of the other superpower's orbit, regardless of whether they were dictatorships or believed in democracy.

The end of the cold war and the collapse of the centrally planned economies accelerated a worldwide process of convergence of political-economic systems. The end of the conflict between the First and Second Worlds also marked the end of the so-called Third World as a political and economic identity. The term "non-alignment" has become obsolete now that there is neither a "communist bloc" nor "free world" to be aligned with. Long-standing ideological differences are evaporating. The trend is towards a single world system in which participation in the dynamism of world trade and economic modernization counts for more than the old political dividing lines. Traditional left-right paradigms are less in evidence. Classical oppositions between "plan" and "market", government action and private initiative, no longer represent alternative political-economic orders but variants of a generally applicable basic pattern of an organized market economy. Capitalism's 19th- and 20th-century competitors – fascism, socialism and communism – are gone as systems. Whether they will re-emerge as ideas with a significant following remains to be seen. The social welfare state, which some saw as a "third way" between capitalism and socialism, is in a serious crisis and seems to have ceased to be a viable alternative. Some have even characterized this triumph of the market as the "end of history".

Globalization has certainly brought progress and new opportunities. The world infant mortality rate has been reduced by more than half over the last 30 years. People on average live 17 years longer; and between 1960 and 1993, the difference in life expectancy between North and South was more than halved, from 23 years to 11 years. Combined primary and secondary school enrolment has more than doubled. Improved communication technologies have helped solidarity networks to operate more effectively and made possible the expansion of alternative "fair trade" networks.

On the other hand, more than one billion people in the South still lack access to basic health and education, safe drinking water and adequate nutrition. Despite growing global wealth, one person in three lives in poverty. Besides being morally unacceptable, this is an explosive situation if only because poor people, through improved communication technologies, are becoming ever more aware of how richer people live.

Thus globalization is a two-edged sword, bringing benefits to some and misery to others. Let us look more closely at some of the features of this process.

Competition

One of the hallmarks of globalization is increased and almost ruthless competition. No one would deny that competition can sometimes be very useful. It promotes innovations, stimulates production of better goods and services and helps to achieve an efficient use of resources. Human nature has room for both competition and cooperation, and economic practice should also allow for both: competition in appropriate areas, always controlled against trickery and manipulation, cooperative arrangements where that encourages the best contributions of all partners, and both in a framework of democratic accountability that enables others to step in whenever things go badly wrong.[2]

Lately, however, there is a tendency to give competition the status of a universal credo, an ideology, a solution for nearly every social ill. Is there high unemployment? The answer is more competition and growth. Schools and universities have to adopt more competitive systems to make them more suitable for industry and commerce. Technological research should aim at making industry more competitive. The World Economic Forum and the Institute for Management Development in Lausanne, Switzerland, even publish an annual World Competitiveness Index, which uses 300 criteria to measure the competitive power of national economies.

This focus on competition promotes a one-dimensional view of human nature and human relationships. That part of human nature which values cooperation is neglected at best, and devaluated as "soft", "unrealistic" and "inefficient" at worst. In this arrogantly reductionist view of human nature, the logic of the winner becomes the norm for success, the weak are excluded and the victims are blamed for their lack of competitiveness. If competition crowds out attention to the common good, it becomes a destructive force, pitting people against each other and against nature, sacrificing what is most vulnerable in creation.

What we consider as the optimal mix between competition and cooperation will have something to do with how we see human nature. So, for example, while awareness of human sin characterizes all Christian theologies, various traditions emphasize this in different ways. There is the Orthodox position, which considers people basically good but tempted to do evil. There is the Roman Catholic teaching according to which human beings tend towards good but are also capable of evil. And there is the rigorously Calvinistic view reflected in the Heidelberg Catechism, which says that human beings are altogether unable to do good and prone to do evil. In assessing particular economic systems and policies, those who believe in the basic goodness of human nature may be inclined to leave more room for individual freedom than those who have less confidence in the tendency of human beings to act justly.

Privatization, deregulation, liberalization

The emphasis on competition goes hand in hand with a trend to limit the economic role of the state through privatization, deregulation and liberalization. In the South, these policies often grow out of the "structural adjustment" measures adopted, on the insistence of the International Monetary Fund and the World Bank, in the aftermath of the debt crisis of the 1980s. One objective was to promote the integration of Southern economies into the world economy. Northern countries, notably the USA under President Reagan and the UK under Prime Minister Thatcher, started to reshape their economies in the same direction. The basic idea was the less government intervention in economic life, the better. Government "meddling" spoils the market, distorts competition and promotes inefficiency and waste. Without doubt there is much truth in such arguments – until they are elevated to a credo.

Privatization may serve as an example. Governments of all kinds – left, right and centre – across the globe are currently engaged in the wholesale privatization of state-controlled economic sectors and companies as the key policy instrument in the move to more market-based economic systems. In 1992 alone, state-owned firms worth US$69 billion in nearly 50 countries passed into private hands, bringing the total since 1985 to US$328 billion. In the South, privatization began slowly in the 1980s, but the pace has accelerated and by the early 1990s there had been over 1500 divestitures in the South and a further 2700 in the transition economies of Eastern Europe and central Asia.

In assessing this drive towards more and more privatization, it must be recognized that governments and business influence each other in many direct and indirect ways. So intricate are relations between them that it is often misleading to talk of two "sectors", the public and the private. Public producers produce private goods and services, and private producers produce public goods and services. Most production processes are a mixture of both. Hugh Stretton gives an example from the Cooper Basin in South Australia. A private company buys the right to extract public natural gas. They send the gas through a public pipeline to another private company with a public franchise, which sends it, this time through a private pipe, to a private brickworks. There it is mixed with private clay and public electricity to make bricks. These are transported by private truck on public roads to some public land, where a private builder is constructing houses for a public housing agency – which will in turn sell them to private citizens. To pay for these houses, the buyers will use their own private savings in a private bank, but will also take out a first mortgage derived from other people's private savings in a state bank, and a second mortgage from the public housing agency, which is using for that purpose the commercial profits from its past public housing operations.[3] How can we sort out the public from the private sector? Should we have fewer public hospitals using more privately produced hardware and software? Fewer public roads to carry more private cars? Less public education using more privately produced educational materials? Fewer police officers to protect more private wealth?

What lies behind the present wave of privatizations? Generally, when governments sell their assets, two overriding aims are involved: (1) to shrink the state, in pursuit of greater economic efficiency through more competition; (2) to raise cash to curb a deficit in the public sector. Do privatizations lead to greater economic efficiency? The answer is: it depends. If a public monopoly is sold, it will simply create a highly profitable private monopoly. But monopolies are not usually very economically efficient, precisely because they lack the stimulus of competition. Thus to promote economic efficiency, privatization must be accompanied by an adequate legal regulatory framework – which means more government regulation rather than less. This in turn will probably reduce the price the private sector is willing to pay for the enterprise because it reduces profits. And while selling off a public enterprise will bring the government a high one-time income, it may lose the annual profits such a company could generate. If the public company is sold to foreign investors, part of the profits may be transferred abroad while control over the economic sector in question will diminish.

A more profound question is whether economic efficiency is all that matters. What are the social effects of privatizing health care, education and public transport? Will poor people have more or less access to these services? What accompanying measures are needed to protect the vulnerable? Questions like these remind us that simple ideological recipes are not adequate when approaching complex issues.

"Triadization"

Not all parts of the world are participating in the globalizing economy on an equal footing. There are three regions in which globalization is most apparent, and some would argue that "triadization" is a more precise term than globalization for what is actually happening. The Triad is formed by Europe, especially those countries which are members of the European Union; North America, especially the free-trade zone of NAFTA (the USA, Canada and Mexico); and the "Pacific Rim", notably Japan, the "Four Tigers" (Hong Kong, Taiwan, Singapore and Korea) and probably Malaysia, Thailand and Indonesia – with China as a special case, given its double-digit growth figures over the past decade.

The poorest countries, with 20 percent of the world's population, saw their share of world trade fall from 4 percent in 1960 to less than 1 percent in 1990. They receive a meagre 0.2 percent of the world's commercial lending. According to the 1996 United Nations *Human Development Report*, while private investment flows to Southern countries increased between 1970 and 1994 from US$5 billion to US$173 billion, three-quarters of this went to just ten countries, mostly in East and Southeast Asia and Latin America.

More than 80 percent of international capital flows take place between Triad countries. In 1980, the whole group of so-called developing countries received 55 percent of global capital flows and provided 14 percent; ten years later both figures had fallen to 2 percent. Of the 4200 strategic alliances formed between companies during the 1980s, 92 percent were between corporations in Japan, the European Union and North America. In 1980, the world's 102 poorest countries accounted for 7.9 percent of goods exported and 9 percent of imports worldwide. Ten years later this had dwindled to 1.4 percent and 4.9 percent respectively, while the share of the Triad countries increased from 54.8 percent to 64 percent of exports and from 59.5 percent to 63.8 percent of imports.

This "triadization" creates a two-track world economy: the Triad countries are in the fast lane of economic dynamism, and the other countries, notably those in Sub-Saharan Africa, are in the slow lane – with the distance between the two growing. This duality enhances the polarization of the global economy. The "global village" is becoming a village with rapidly extending slums.[4]

Inequality and exclusion

Of the global Gross Domestic Product (GDP) of US$23 trillion in 1993, only US$5 trillion was produced in the South, where nearly 80 percent of the world's people live – and the gap is widening. But the gap between rich and poor is also growing in individual countries – and not only in the South. The polarization between rich and poor is not simply a North-South issue. While the poorest 40 percent of the world's population are almost all inhabitants of the South, it is estimated that one-third of the wealthiest 20 percent of the world population lives in the South. Brazil has the most unequal distribution of income: the richest 20 percent of the population receives 26 times the income of the poorest 20 percent.

Statistics documenting this wide and growing gap can be multiplied. In the South, 33 percent of the population, 1.3 billion people, receive less than US$1 per day. The combined worth of the world's 358 billionaires – US$760 billion – is equal to the total combined annual income of the world's poorest 2.5 billion people. In the countries of the Organization for Economic Cooperation and Development (OECD), where the average annual income per person is US$20,000, more than 100 million people live below the official poverty line, some 35 million are unemployed and more than 5 million are homeless.

Between 1973 and 1994, the real per capita GDP in the USA rose 33 percent, yet hourly wages fell 14 percent. By the end of 1994 real wages were back to where they had been in the late 1950s, though family income continues to grow because people work longer hours and more women work. While an ever-higher proportion of people in the US are working harder for less money, corporate profits have risen by an annual average of 13 percent and the salaries of corporate executive officers have skyrocketed.[5]

In the countries of Eastern Europe and the former Soviet Union, per capita income has fallen on average by a third since the mid-1980s. People in these countries enjoy more political freedom, but the erosion of purchasing power, inequality in income distribution and unemployment have increased poverty, rates of violent crimes and malnutrition, while the deterioration of the position of women and lower standards of education have undercut many earlier achievements. The decision of the Russian government to remove state control over prices in early 1992 led to a nearly fivefold increase in producer prices. The liberalization of imports put more products on the shelves in the shops, but very few people can afford to buy them. During the four years following the introduction of this shock therapy, industrial production fell by 46 percent and GDP by 42 percent. These problems have been compounded by a massive capital flight, estimated at US\$100 billion from 1992 to 1994, far more than the US\$19.4 billion in Western direct investment and official aid during the same period. A 1994 report found that 70 to 80 percent of private banks and businesses in major Russian cities were forced to make payments of 10 to 20 percent of their revenues to organized crime.

Developments in the South follow a similar pattern. In 1981 the share of the national income of the richest 10 percent of Thais was 17 times that of the poorest 10 percent; by 1992, the multiple was 38. In Mexico, which has seven dollar-billionaires (as many as the United Kingdom), 16 percent of the population – 13 million people – are officially classified as living in "extreme poverty" and another 23.6 million as "poor". Incomes in Nigeria have fallen by a quarter since the mid-1970s. In Sierra Leone, where tens of thousands of people displaced by civil war struggle to keep hope alive in "temporary camps", the average person lives 42 years and per capita income is US$200 a year. In Niger, average school attendance is barely one year, life expectancy is 45 years and per capita annual income is US$310. Africa as a whole includes 33 of the world's 50 poorest countries. The combined GNP of the entire continent south of the Sahara is less than that of the Netherlands; and Sub-Saharan Africa is the only region in the world likely to experience an increase in absolute poverty over the next decade.

Unemployment, wages and lowering standards

Unemployment is a more and more serious problem in almost all societies. In OECD countries, some 35 million people are out of work, and many more are working part-time but would prefer or need full-time employment. Women and youth are especially affected. In Australia, 77 percent of the women are unemployed; in some European countries more than 60 percent of young people who have left school are without a job. In Bulgaria and Hungary, where the Communist system virtually guaranteed a job for everyone, unemployment ballooned to 30 percent. While reliable employment statistics for many Southern countries are hard to obtain, there is no doubt that many people are unemployed or underemployed.

Even in the US, where the economy is growing and unemployment is relatively low, job security is declining. Job security is notoriously low in the informal sector – and in many Southern countries, it is the informal economy which is growing. In Latin America it provides employment for 57 percent of the workforce. Between 1980 and 1993, 82 of every 100 new jobs in Latin America were generated in the informal sector. Fierce competition drives down labour costs and creates a growing demand for flexibility, leading to precarious and often abusive working conditions. The globalization of the economy is creating a two-tier labour market: a shrinking stable and skilled workforce and a growth in the number of temporary and precarious jobs, mainly occupied by women.

The differentials between the highest and the lowest wages are growing. According to the OECD's 1996 Employment Outlook, wage inequality is generally higher in countries with deregulated labour markets. A cut in the minimum wage for young workers will reduce wages at the bottom while leaving pay at the top untouched. Governments accept weaker job-protection in the belief that this will increase employment, because companies will be inclined to hire more workers if wages are lower and it is easier to fire them. Low unemployment figures in the United States are quoted to prove this thesis. However, evidence shows that the jobs thus created often are poor-quality jobs.

Labour-market "flexibility" translates into companies demanding longer hours from their workers while reserving the right to sack them whenever management feels that it is necessary to increase profits. The world's 500 largest corporations shed 4.4 million jobs between 1980 and 1993 – while increasing their sales by 1.4 times, their assets by 2.3 times, and compensation for their corporate executive officers by 6.1 times. These corporations, which employ only 0.05 percent of the world's population, control 25 percent of the world's output and 70 percent of world trade. In January 1996 the US communications giant AT&T announced that it would cut 40,000 jobs – after the company had posted two years of record profits (nearly US$9 billion) and while its chairman had an annual salary of US$14 million. Unfortunately this is not an isolated event but part of a general trend.

The old assumption that economic growth will automatically expand employment and wages is increasingly questioned. The phenomenon of "jobless growth" has appeared in most industrial countries, where unemployment has been rising despite economic growth. But this phenomenon is not limited to the North. In Ghana, for example, the GDP grew by 4.8 percent between 1986 and 1991 but employment dropped by more than 13 percent.[6]

Furthermore, the conventional belief that unemployment creates an unfavourable business climate also seems less true. When official statistics in January 1997 showed that the US unemployment rate had fallen to one of its lowest levels in recent decades, share prices *dropped*: what was good news for the people turned out to be a bad sign for Wall Street. It was long assumed that when more people are working, consumption will increase, requiring more production and leading to increased sales, higher economic growth, improved prospects for the corporate world and, consequently, higher share prices. Today, however, stock exchanges are dominated by speculative capital. Those operating with such capital fear that lower unemployment could cause the economy to overheat, resulting in inflation and increased interest rates, leading to lower share prices and thus reduced profitability for their financial investments.

Expansion of the market beyond the boundaries of the nation-state effectively places market power outside the reach of national governments. This has been an important consequence of the structural adjustment programmes imposed by international financial institutions and the trade agreements negotiated under the World Trade Organization. Globalization thus transfers governance decisions from governments – which at least in theory represent the interests of all citizens in their countries – to the dominant institutions of the market and the international organizations, in which the most powerful nations have a decisive influence. The principle of national sovereignty is coming under severe challenge, and some observers believe that we are witnessing the beginning of the end of national systems.

In global markets, economic activities tend to migrate to where the highest profits can be made and restrictions on business activities are the lowest. With unemployment high, governments are of course eager to attract economic activity from elsewhere; and to compete with others they are ready to deregulate the labour market (for example, by lowering the minimum wage), decrease taxes and reduce regulations for business. Of course, if they reduce their tax income, they will also have to reduce their public spending – which explains why the social welfare state is threatening to break down. The logic of this is explained by Paul Craig Roberts, a former US assistant secretary of the treasury:

> In a global economy, capital will flow to areas where returns are highest and away from those where it is savaged by taxes, regulations and tort liabilities.
> So the United States has no choice but to stop building welfare and entitlement dependencies that it can no longer afford, and to return to the small-government era that permitted wave after wave of penniless immigrants to be absorbed into the economic life of a thriving nation...
> If the United States, a welfare state grown soft and fat, is to survive in a competitive post-socialist world, it must privatize Social Security and health care, abolish welfare and cease to tax human and physical capital.[7]

Such logic pits localities against one another in a scramble to offer higher subsidies, more generous exemptions from corporate tax, and lower environmental and employment standards. Similarly, workers are pitted against one another in efforts to push wages down.

While the era of national economic regulation is ending, the age of global regulation is not yet here. Where there are elements of control, these are largely Northern-dominated. No agreement can be reached on questions like who should regulate, what should be regulated, how it should be regulated. The discussion of a code of conduct for activities of transnational corporations is a case in point. Such a code has been debated for more than 20 years but no progress has been made.

Globalization, markets and democracy

With direct government control over economic activities within their own national boundaries (for example, controls on capital movements) becoming less and less effective as private-sector economic agents can more and more easily evade their impact, governments have few alternatives to pursuing market-oriented economic policies. Maintaining "market credibility" is paramount – and a government is considered "credible" if it pursues policies in accordance with what markets believe to be "sound", that is, policies which create an enabling environment for the private sector and the efficient operation of the market economy.

Even if governments would like to be more in control, they find it difficult. When the British merchant bank Barings collapsed in February 1995 after amassing US$1.4 billion of trading losses, British government regulators admitted that they did not "really understand" Barings Securities, its trading arm.

Is the present process of globalization compatible with democracy, social justice and the social welfare state? If democratically elected governments feel obliged to obey impersonal market forces, who will be the guardian of social justice? How can citizens participate in decision-making processes which shape their future? There is an important tension between democracy and the emerging global market. Democracy believes in an equal distribution of political power based on "one person, one vote", while the global market operates on the principle that it is the duty of the economically capable to drive the economically incapable out of business. At present, the egalitarian forces of democracy seem to be losing out to the cold-blooded forces which preach the "survival of the fittest" in a global market.

The development of the massive international capital market over the past two decades illustrates the erosion of the sovereignty of nation-states. In 1973, typical daily foreign exchange trading amounted to only about US$10-20 billion; and ten years later it was still only about US$60 billion. By 1992, however, some US$900 billion was changing hands in the foreign-exchange market every day. It is estimated that in 1996 the daily turnover was well over US$1.2 trillion – about the same amount as the total currency reserves of all the world's central banks. The total stock of financial assets traded in the global capital market in 1992 was US$35 trillion, equivalent to twice the GDP of the OECD countries; and it is forecast to increase to US$83 trillion in 2000, three times the GDP of the OECD economies.

It is not difficult to see that no individual government is in a position to control this vast pool of financial resources. Even an organization like the International Monetary Fund (IMF) cannot handle this situation, as was illustrated during the Mexico crisis. The Mexican bailout required more funds than the IMF was allowed to lend, and the United States had to come to the rescue. The behaviour of this vast pool of capital sets the parameters for the policies of national governments rather than the other way round. This means that democracy is undermined.

Globalization and taxes

From time immemorial, people have tried to escape taxes. Globalization has made this easier, for at least three reasons. The first is that many firms have more freedom over where to locate, and can thus more easily choose to operate in countries where taxes are low. Activities that require only a computer terminal, telephone and modem can be located almost anywhere. Moreover, the expansion of business conducted over the Internet makes it difficult to track and hence tax these transactions.

Second, globalization makes it hard to decide and control where a company should pay taxes. As we shall see later, the system of transfer-pricing enables transnational corporations to pay inflated prices for components or services imported from a subsidiary in a low-tax country, thus moving its taxable profits to that country and reducing its tax bill. It is no coincidence that subsidiaries of US companies report higher profit margins in low-tax countries than in high-tax ones. Of course this is not a new phenomenon, but the scale of the problem is growing. In 1970 a typical large US company earned 10-20 percent of its income from abroad; now many earn at least half their profits outside the United States.

The third reason why globalization is a problem for taxation has to do with the mobility of skilled professional workers. In May 1997, several large Swedish companies said they were considering moving out of the country because of high taxes. Their complaint was not about the rate of corporate tax but about high personal income taxes, which make it difficult to recruit skilled employees. But even if highly skilled individuals do not move abroad, they often earn a growing slice of their income from overseas, for example by consultancy work. Such income is relatively easy to hide from the tax authorities. Taxing personal savings also becomes harder when these can be zapped electronically from one side of the globe to the other.

As a result, there is a shift everywhere from taxing capital towards taxing less mobile factors of production. The corporate world reaps the benefits. In general, firms are not only subject to lower tax rates, but may also be offered additional tax breaks or are even public subsidies to attract their business. In order to lure a BMW auto plant, the US state of South Carolina offered tax concessions. BMW then said it favoured a 1000-acre tract on which a number of middle-class homes were located. So the state bought the 140 properties and leased the site to BMW for one dollar a year. In addition, the taxpayers of South Carolina picked up the costs of recruiting, screening and training workers for the new plant.

The crisis in Asia

In 1998, after three decades of whirlwind growth, a severe crisis hit the booming economies of the Southeast Asian "Tigers". It was forecast that their economies would grow more slowly in the coming period – about 1 percent a year – than those of the rich industrial countries. China and Japan might be able to achieve higher rates, but Indonesia, South Korea and Thailand, with previous growth rates of 7-8 percent, would suffer outright recessions. Unemployment was expected to triple, reaching 6 to 10 percent. What happened?

To a certain extent these countries could be described as victims of their own success. Years of breathtaking growth had attracted vast inflows of foreign capital during the 1990s, reaching as much as 17 percent of GDP in Malaysia in 1993 and 13 percent in Thailand in 1995.[8] The liberalization of financial markets had allowed these high infusions of foreign capital, making these economies highly dependent on foreign investment. But the lion's share of this foreign investment was not oriented to long-term productive activities but went into real estate and the stock market. The result was a massive oversupply of residential and commercial properties from Bangkok to Jakarta. When foreign investors recognized that this real estate glut meant they were sitting on a bubble, they panicked and began to withdraw their money. The huge inflows soon turned into huge outflows.

But foreign capital movements are not the sole explanation for the Asian crisis. The countries affected have also been known for opacity, cronyism and poor regulation. The combination of these internal and external factors highlights the weakness of a model of development based on accelerated integration into the global economy. Financial liberalization and reliance on short-term foreign capital flows combined with poor regulation is disastrous. Rather than wholesale liberalization of financial markets, capital flows should be controlled and participation in globalization should be selective. In this respect, Chile is often cited as an example. It discourages volatile capital flows resulting from short-term investments and speculation by requiring that 30 percent of all inflows be deposited at the central bank for one year without interest. Moreover, any foreign money coming into Chile must stay in the country for at least a year.

Some other effects

Besides growing concentration of power, a widening gap between rich and poor, downward pressure on wages and social standards, high unemployment, the crisis of the welfare state and the erosion of national sovereignty, globalization is accompanied by other features as well, of which we shall mention three.

First, global marketing of consumer products through the media is effectively promoting a commercialized homogenization of cultures. While the world's more than 1.2 billion television sets help to spread knowledge and understanding, they are also a conduit for cultural domination through the values they transmit. The United States annually exports more than 120,000 hours of television programming to Europe alone, and this global trade is growing by more than 15 percent a year.

A second point to be made is that globalized markets should not be equated with *free* markets. Goods, services and capital may increasingly move unhindered around the globe, but labour and people cannot. Almost no government is inclined to liberalize the market for labour and open its borders to workers from other countries. An important exception is the European Union, but labour mobility there is restricted to the citizens of its own member countries.

Nevertheless, according to the International Labour Organization, there are some 70 million migrant workers around the world. The most popular destinations are North America, Europe, the Gulf states and East Asia, but there is also an increase in South-to-South migration, particularly in Asia. It is also in Asia that the feminization of migration flows is most evident; the ratio from the Philippines is twelve women migrants to every man. Poverty, population growth, civil, ethnic and religious conflicts, and environmental degradation all add to migratory pressures.[9]

Most migrants have few if any skills. Considered as second-class labour, they are usually employed in the unpleasant tasks that the nationals of the host country would rather not do. Typically, they earn less for the same work and face discrimination in hiring, promotion, social security and job security. They are also easy targets of popular discontent. In industrialized countries, nationals see them as rivals who have come to "steal" jobs or homes. They are accused of sponging off the social security system and contributing to a rising crime rate. In fact, several studies in Germany and Switzerland have shown that immigrant workers contribute more to the host country than they cost it, particularly in terms of social security.

The third observation is that the forces of globalization or triadization are accompanied by a renewed emphasis on national or ethnic identity. With the end of colonization, the names of countries often changed in the years after the second world war, but the borders remained largely the same. With the end of the centrally planned economic systems in Central and Eastern Europe, however, borders too are changing. Only two countries became one – East and West Germany – while some 20 new countries have appeared. The former Soviet Union split into 15 separate countries; the former Yugoslavia into five (one of which, Bosnia, is in effect divided), and the Czech Republic and Slovakia decided to form two countries.

Other movements for self-determination or varying degrees of autonomy can be found in Spain (the Basques and Catalans), France (Corsica and Brittany), the United Kingdom (Scotland and Wales), Italy (the Northern League) and Canada (Quebec). These processes of fission run alongside developments towards fusion, especially through the creation of regional free-trade zones. Economic forces undermine national sovereignty while stimulating regional integration.

Many people consider these seemingly contradictory processes as confusing and threatening. Together with the process of cultural homogenization and the resistance to it, this may help to explain the resurgence of religious fundamentalism and intolerance in some places. Historically, uncertainty has given rise to religious fundamentalism; today individuals try to escape the economic uncertainty of the "real world" by retreating into the certainty of a religious world where they are told that if they follow the prescribed rules, they will be saved. Often, this is combined with a striving for ethnic separation. The emphasis on ethnicity can be a survival strategy and promote group solidarity. But if it is misused and manipulated for political goals, the effects can be disastrous.

In a well-known essay later expanded into a book, the Harvard political scientist Samuel Huntington predicted that the 21st century would be one of conflicts between cultures or "civilizations" rather than between ideologies or social classes.[10] In particular, Huntington predicted an escalating clash between the West and Islam. The key question would not be "Whose side are you on?" but "What are you?" However, Huntington's thesis is clearly inadequate. Ethnic and religious divisions do not always coincide: Muslims have killed Muslims in Afghanistan, Iraq and Algeria; and Christian fundamentalists have shot doctors who carry out abortions, derailed trains and blown up a government building in the US, whose administrators and politicians are overwhelmingly Christian. In Israel, a Jewish fundamentalist shot a Jewish prime minister; Buddhist fundamentalists released nerve gas in the Tokyo subways aiming at fellow Buddhists. "What are you?" is evidently an important question – though "Muslim", "Christian", "Buddhist", "Hindu" or "Jew" is an insufficient answer. And in a globalizing world, with growing gaps between rich and poor, "Whose side are you on?" is still a relevant question.

Globalization of justice

Simultaneous with economic globalization, we are witnessing what might be called a "globalization from below". Technological advances such as electronic mail are enabling new international networks of people's movements to exchange information on issues and organize international advocacy campaigns. The development of alternative or fair trade schemes, which we shall look at in a later chapter, is another example of globalization from below.

Cooperative globalization, rather than globalization built on competition, is therefore also a feature of our era. It may stimulate the notion of global citizenship at a time in which the role of the nation-state is being reduced. Such cooperation is based on the recognition that global citizenship can exist only if it is rooted in local citizenship.

Globalization cannot be wished away. Despite the many negative features connected with it, there are also new opportunities for those who work towards the globalization of justice and solidarity. The challenge is to exploit such possibilities through selective participation in globalization processes, and to promote more inclusive rather than exclusive globalization.

NOTES

[1] Cf. Reginald Dale, "'Globalization' Does a World of Good", *International Herald Tribune*, 22 March 1996.

[2] Cf. *Christian Faith and the World Economy Today: A Study Document from the World Council of Churches*, Geneva, WCC, 1992, p.37.

[3] Hugh Stretton, *Political Essays*, Melbourne, Georgian House Publishers, 1987, p.20.

[4] *A World of Difference: A New Framework for Development Cooperation in the 1990s*, a policy document of the Dutch ministry for development, The Hague, 1991, p.35.

[5] On these trends cf. Lester Thurow, *The Future of Capitalism: How Today's Economic Forces Will Shape Tomorrow's World*, London, Nicholas Brealey, 1996, p.24.

[6] UN Development Programme, *Human Development Report 1996*, p.57.

[7] Quoted in the *International Herald Tribune*, 5 Dec. 1994.

[8] *The Economist*, 7 March 1998.

[9] Cf. the recent statement on uprooted people by the WCC Central Committee, *A Moment To Choose*, Geneva, WCC, 1996.

[10] Samuel Huntington, "The Clash of Civilizations", *Foreign Affairs*, Vol. 72, no.3, summer 1993, pp.2-26; *The Clash of Civilizations and the Remaking of World Order*, New York, Simon & Schuster, 1996.

3. International Trade

"Free trade," wrote Richard Cobden in 1857, "is God's diplomacy, and there is no other certain way of uniting people in the bonds of peace."[1] If that is so, many politicians today can indeed be regarded as God's ambassadors, since scarcely a week passes without someone somewhere announcing that trade must be made freer still. When the Uruguay Round of the General Agreement on Tariffs and Trade (GATT) talks ended in December 1993, some 100 countries promised to cut tariffs, dismantle non-tariff barriers to trade and liberalize trade in services.

When GATT was established in 1947, only 23 countries took part in the negotiations, and the first round of talks finished within a year. The eighth and last round lasted more than seven years. During this 50-year period, the average tariff has fallen from almost 40 percent to around 4 percent. This has had a profound effect on the world economy and has greatly stimulated the process of globalization. During the 1990s, international trade has grown faster than world output, showing that national economies are becoming ever more closely linked.

A significant outcome of the Uruguay Round was the creation of the World Trade Organization (WTO), a new institution to administer and implement multilateral trade agreements, act as a forum for new trade negotiations, resolve trade disputes and cooperate with other international institutions in global policy-making. The WTO has 132 members; and another 30 countries, including China and Russia, would like to join. Under GATT, any member could veto the verdict of a panel set up to rule on a quarrel – even if it was a party to the dispute. WTO panels are stricter. They must report within nine months and their decisions can be overturned only by consensus. This gives the impression that the WTO is a more democratic organization than, for example, the IMF or the World Bank, where voting is based on the economic wealth and power of a member state. It is however a worrying sign that the WTO's general council decided in 1996 that it would not develop any formal relationships with nongovernmental organizations (NGOs), thus excluding an important part of civil society from any meetings of WTO standing bodies for settling disputes, trade and development, and trade and environment.

The effects of the Uruguay Round

The Uruguay Round agreements on Trade Related Property Rights (TRIPs) have substantially increased the extent to which Southern countries are required to respect patents and copyrights held outside their territories. This will increase costs for the South while reducing its access to certain technologies. Those who benefit are the holders of intellectual property rights, which are overwhelmingly transnational corporations (TNCs) in the North. The danger is that the TRIPs agreement will perpetuate the concentration of ownership and control of intellectual property in the North.

Large drug-producing TNCs who were a driving force behind the TRIPs deal, argue that patents are essential to reward innovation, and that without them drugs like those to fight AIDS or Alzheimer's disease might never be developed. They argue that good intellectual property protection will eventually be profitable in Southern countries and attract more foreign investment. The opponents of TRIPs point to the fact that patent-holders are usually based in the North while patent-dodgers tend to be firms in the South. Although the latter are by no means charitable organizations, their products are cheaper than branded patented ones. If firms enjoy monopoly rights through the patent system, the critics argue, prices are likely to go up and poor people will not be able to afford the products.

India, for example, imposes strict controls on drug prices, whereas in Pakistan, where products are granted patents, prices are up to ten times higher. There are many examples of drugs made by TNCs costing more in the South than in their home markets. Even if medicines do not become more expensive, TRIPs still cost poor countries money; an estimated US$5 billion a year flows to US pharmaceutical companies alone. Moreover, an Indian committee working on patent laws has estimated that most of the country's 10,000 local manufacturers, which produce 70 percent of the country's drugs, would eventually go out of business as a result of the TRIPs agreement. Medicines monopolized by their inventors would replace the drugs prescribed today.

World trade in textiles and clothing has been governed since 1964 by a range of restrictions under the Multi-Fibre Arrangement (MFA). This has been extremely disadvantageous for certain Southern countries which rely heavily on the export of textiles and clothing. The Uruguay Round agreement to phase out the MFA over a ten-year period was thus an important achievement, but Northern countries have dragged their feet and are postponing the implementation of the agreement until the very last moment. Commitment to free trade evidently has its limits when the interests of Northern industries are at stake.

Even after the Uruguay Round, agriculture remains the most heavily protected sector of international trade. The measures include a wide array of price supports, production limits and producer subsidies. While these are justifiable if they are directed to the most marginal farmers, protect rural communities and take account of environmental concerns, they are doubtful when they are aimed at large farmers and support unsustainable farming methods.

The cuts in domestic and export farm subsidies mandated by the Uruguay Round will in the short run lead to a higher food import bill for Southern countries. This is aggravated by a decrease in food aid, forcing low-income food-deficit countries to import food commercially. The ACP countries (in Africa, the Caribbean and the Pacific), which as former colonies of member states of the European Union now enjoy favourable treatment of their agricultural products under the Lomé Convention, are likely to see these privileges reduced when the fourth Lomé Convention expires in 2000. The combination of these effects may lead to a worsening of balance of payments difficulties.

However, while consumers in the South, especially in urban areas, will be faced with higher prices, Southern farmers who no longer have to compete with under-priced imports from Northern countries will have an incentive to increase production. In the end, more food security may be the result. On the other hand, there is a snag in the agreement to reduce subsidies for agricultural exports: an exception is made for food aid. It remains to be seen to what extent this will be detrimental for food security in the South.

The effects of the Uruguay Round will differ from country to country. One study has concluded that the world as a whole will be at least $213 billion a year richer by 2002 as a result of the Uruguay Round, but that Sub-Saharan Africa will be $2.6 billion poorer. Christian Aid in the United Kingdom reports that the relatively developed countries of East Asia (including China) and Latin America will benefit more from the Uruguay Round liberalization than the low-income developing countries and the least-developed countries. It endorses a proposal by WTO Director-General Renato Ruggiero that Northern countries offer zero-tariff access to the least developed countries. This would not be a major change in the international trading environment because the least developed countries account for only 0.3 percent of world exports.[2]

Even this proposal would not solve all the problems of the least-developed countries, many of which depend for their exports on a small number of commodities. Prices of primary products are not only more unstable than those of manufactured goods which are produced in the richer countries, but have also tended to move downwards in real terms over the past several decades. Pressed to raise foreign exchange to service their external debt, poor countries have felt the need to sell their primary commodities competitively on the world market. As many countries did this at the same time, prices went down and income declined. This was further aggravated when recession in the 1980s reduced demand in the North. Moreover, the importance of some primary commodities has declined because of technological developments. Satellites have replaced copper wire, plastics are now used instead of rubber in many products and artificial sweeteners take the place of cane sugar. Such substitutions further marginalize countries heavily dependent on primary products. Thus it is scarcely a surprise that the poorest countries, with 20 percent of the world's population, saw their share of world trade fall from 4 percent in 1960 to less than 1 percent in 1990.[3]

Social and environmental clauses

A highly contentious issue in the WTO is that of the so-called trade-related clauses, particularly in two areas: social clauses and environmental clauses.

The former are provisions that would make the level of access to world markets conditional on recognizing fundamental workers' rights – freedom of association, collective bargaining, minimum age, equal remuneration and prohibition of discrimination and forced labour. Introducing social clauses would make it possible to curtail the import of products from countries where labour conditions do not meet certain minimum standards.

The pressure to include labour standards in international trade policy is not only rooted in concern about the situation of workers. It can also be motivated by a wish to reduce the competitive edge in attracting foreign investment and keeping export prices low which some countries are believed to derive from labour which is cheap because basic rights are not respected and efforts to secure them suppressed. While social clauses could be an instrument to stop the downward spiral of labour standards, they would apply only to those who work in the export sectors of an economy and not address the often much worse labour conditions of those working for companies which produce for the domestic market. Trade sanctions and social clauses are not appropriate or sufficient mechanisms to uphold labour standards throughout a country; and social clauses may penalize a country according to the size of its export sector rather than the extent of overall suppression of labour rights.

Fears that social clauses may be misused for protectionist ends have been fuelled by the US decision to stop importing garments made by children under 15. One of the first countries to be hit was Bangladesh. In 1995-96, the garment industry was responsible for almost 62 percent of Bangladesh's total exports – worth US$1.94 billion. When garment-makers sent home at least 50,000 children workers as a result of the US decision, some 1.5 million families were affected. Many of the children, who have earned between US$30 and US$40 a month, now earn a meagre income as garbage collectors or as prostitutes.[4] It is no accident that this decision will benefit the US textile and garment industries, but will it solve the problem of child labour?

A 1996 meeting in Kundapur, India, which brought together child workers from 24 countries, was almost unanimous in saying that it is better to address the root causes, notably poverty, than to ban child labour. Of the 250 million child workers in the world, only a small percentage work in the export industry and would therefore be covered by a social clause.

Some have argued that the International Labour Office (ILO), rather than the WTO, should take the lead in implementing and monitoring social clauses, because representation in the ILO includes trade unions and employers organizations as well as governments. Although nearly anything can be considered trade-related, this does not mean that regulation should focus on trade or be given to the WTO to monitor.

The debate around including environmental clauses in the WTO centres on a proposed ban on importing goods produced in an environmentally destructive way. Again the fear is that countries will misuse such a clause to protect their own industries. One example is a ban imposed by the USA on the import of tunafish from Mexico because the driftnet fishing methods were killing dolphins unnecessarily. Even after Mexico improved its fishing methods, as certified by numerous environmental groups, it proved very difficult to lift the ban. In general, Southern countries' fears of "green protectionism" – rules masquerading as environmentalism which would exclude their products from Northern markets – seems valid, though this fear might diminish if rules were carefully drawn to avoid misuse. But rather than banning products produced in a socially and environmentally harmful way, it may be preferable to lower tariffs or otherwise privilege the import of goods produced in a responsible way. Such products could be marked with social and environmental labels to inform the public about the conditions under which they were produced.

Some other issues

• Even apart from the misuse of environmental and social considerations to reintroduce protectionism, the US treatment of its trading relations with Mexico in the context of the North American Free Trade Agreement (NAFTA) illustrates how powerful nations can resist the application of principles of free trade when it is their own economic interests which are at stake. For example, hand-made corn brooms, imported duty-free from Mexico under NAFTA, soon captured 60 percent of the US market. To protect the US industry, in November 1996, the USA slapped three-year quotas and "safeguard" tariffs on these brooms.

While fewer than 400 jobs and $10 million worth of sales were involved, this restrictive action of the USA had a devastating effect on the small town of Cadereyta, capital of the Mexican corn broom industry. Similarly, Mexican tomato-growers have had to accept export prices imposed by the US to avoid punitive anti-dumping charges; and little progress has been achieved in negotiations to lift a ban on Mexican avocados in force since 1914. Nor has the US budged on its refusal to allow Mexican truckers over the border. Under NAFTA it was agreed that, from 1995, trucks would be able to travel freely throughout the border states in both countries. After 12 years they were to be allowed to travel throughout both countries. US trade unions, fearing the loss of jobs to low-wage Mexican drivers, managed to convince the US administration to delay implementation of this agreement.

• An important challenge to the WTO concerns the terms under which China should be brought into the organization. While the WTO can hardly live up to its name without the world's eleventh-biggest exporter, incorporating China presents both technical and political problems. The technical difficulty is to bring the vast "socialist market economy" into line with the WTO's more-or-less free-market principles. Although China has taken steps to liberalize its economy over the past decade, it still maintains many controls which infringe WTO regulations, and the Chinese are determined to keep a protective shroud around some industries that are considered strategic. The political issue centres on China's human rights record. Especially within the US, this issue has created an unusual alliance between protectionists and the human rights activists, which is likely to be strengthened by the fact that China's trade surplus with the USA has become as large as Japan's.

• The original proposal for the Uruguay Round Trade Related Investment Measures (TRIMs) agreement would have extended the rights of foreign investors far beyond the current position in most Southern countries, severely curtailing the ability of governments to regulate the entry, establishment and operations of foreign companies and investors. Due to strong opposition from the South this provision was dropped but it was picked up by the Organization for Economic Cooperation and Development (OECD), which groups 29 rich countries, in negotiations for a Multilateral Agreement on Investment (MAI).

Such an agreement would further liberalization and deregulation by granting foreign firms the same market access and rights to state subsidies as domestic companies. The OECD negotiations on the MAI drew considerable criticism from Southern countries and non-governmental organizations. A dossier on the MAI prepared by the World Council of Churches noted that negotiations for this agreement, which would take away democratic powers from governments while giving new rights to transnational corporations, were being carried on without public participation or debate and excluded the majority of countries in the world. Moreover, the MAI would effectively dismantle existing environmental and social laws. The WCC thus concluded that the MAI was unfair and potentially damaging to the poor countries.[5]

OECD ministers decided at their meeting in April 1998 to adjourn negotiations on the MAI, but it is expected that the issue will surface again in the context of the WTO.

If the MAI were incorporated into it, the WTO would no longer be a "trade organization" but an agency with substantial powers to regulate investments worldwide. This would have serious implications for Southern countries that have found it necessary to regulate foreign investments and to protect local firms. Proponents argue that the MAI would be the best way to promote the entry of foreign investments into the South. Although this cannot be denied, and although under certain circumstances foreign investments can indeed play a relevant and significant role, the MAI would be yet another way to undermine national sovereignty, thereby reducing even further the possibilities for national governments to establish policies aimed at regulating foreign interests according to national priorities and specific situations. It would further strengthen the already powerful position of transnational corporations, an issue to which we turn in the next chapter.

NOTES

[1] Cited in *The Economist*, 7 Dec. 1996.
[2] Cf. Sonali Wickrema and Peter Madden, *The Lands that Time Forgot: The World Trade Organization and Action for the Poorest*, London, Christian Aid, 1996.
[3] UN Development Programme, *Human Development Report 1996*, p.9.
[4] Cf. *Internationale Samenwerking* (The Hague), no.2, Feb. 1997; Consumer Unity and Trust Society (Calcutta), *Briefing Paper*, no. 1, March 1996.
[5] "Dossier I on Multilateral Agreement on Investment", Geneva, WCC, Feb. 1998; see also *License to Loot: The MAI and How to Stop It*, Washington, Friends of the Earth, 1998.

4. Transnational Corporations

With the sovereignty of nation-states eroding and global government nowhere in sight, transnational corporations (TNCs) have taken advantage of this vacuum to become truly global in their reach.

The number of TNCs has grown from around 7000 in 1970 to some 39,000 in 1995. In addition to 270,000 affiliates, TNCs operate through hundreds of thousands of other links such as subcontracts, licencing agreements and strategic alliances between parent companies and other entities. In 1995, the value of foreign direct investments controlled by TNCs reached US$2.7 trillion. The reduction of restrictive measures has greatly contributed to TNC activities; and 106 of the 112 regulatory changes regarding investment in 64 countries in 1995 alone were in the direction of greater liberalization.[1] The TRIPs and TRIMs of the Uruguay Round, discussed in the previous chapter, have further strengthened TNCs' position.

Since 1983, foreign direct investments have grown five times faster than world trade and ten times faster than world output. TNCs now account for two-thirds of the world trade in goods and services. From 1980 to 1992, TNC sales skyrocketed from $2.4 trillion to $5.5 trillion. TNCs own or control 86 percent of the world's land that is cultivated for export crops, control 60 percent of aluminium mining and sell 90 percent of the world's agrochemical products. Some TNCs are financially more powerful than national economies: annual sales of the Royal Dutch/Shell Group oil company are twice New Zealand's gross domestic product (GDP); those of the British tobacco company BAT Industries are equivalent to the GDP of Hungary.[2]

One reason for the increased power and reach of TNCs is mergers and take-overs, a key strategy for establishing production facilities abroad to enhance international competitiveness. Between 1988 and 1995 the value of such transactions doubled to US$229 billion – drastically reshaping the corporate landscape and concentrating economic power in certain key sectors in fewer hands. In 1996 the merger of two US manufacturers, Boeing and McDonnell-Douglas, reduced the number of suppliers of large commercial aircraft to basically two – Boeing and the European Airbus. The same year saw the largest merger ever, between the Swiss pharmaceutical firms Ciba-Geigy and Sandoz, valued at US$36.3 billion. In France, Axa SA and UAP SA merged to create the world's second-largest insurance company.

What are the driving forces behind this trend? For one thing, take-overs provide ready access to established markets and distribution networks and sometimes offer the opportunity to acquire new technology. The market position of a corporation is obviously strengthened if competitors are eliminated. High costs for research and development constitute another reason for pooling resources. And the development or acquisition of sophisticated production technologies requires huge amounts of money, which may make further concentration necessary.

TNC activities are concentrated in a few countries. Two-thirds of the total TNC investment inflows in 1995 went to only ten countries, while the smallest 100 recipient countries received only 1 percent. The world's 100 largest TNCs (excluding banking and financial institutions), ranked by foreign assets, are all based in the rich countries. Together, they have roughly $1.4 trillion worth of assets abroad. The share of TNC investment in Sub-Saharan Africa is falling, thereby further marginalizing that region. Foreign direct investment in Central and Eastern Europe is growing, mainly due to privatization of state enterprises. Most of the TNC activities in the South are limited to a small number of countries in Asia and Latin America. Since 1992 China has been the largest Southern recipient of foreign investment.

Why go abroad?

Companies have different reasons for becoming transnational. Those producing consumer goods may cross national borders in search of new markets. Transport costs and tariffs or other trade barriers can make it more profitable to produce goods as close as possible to the place where they are sold. For example, to produce oil barrels in a country faraway from where they will be filled would involve costly transportation of what is mainly air. Corporations outside the European Union may wish to avoid import tariffs by setting up shop within an EU country.

Some corporations go abroad to exploit raw materials: oil companies go to Nigeria, mining companies to Malaysia, logging companies to Brazil. Corporations for whom labour costs are important may look for places where wages are low and trade unions less powerful and more docile. Tax holidays, low taxes and the possibility of remitting large portions of profits to the home country may also encourage a company to establish an affiliate in a certain area. The growth of Export Processing Zones is a case in point; indeed, Hong Kong, Macao and Singapore have turned into Export Processing Countries, and Mauritius and Sri Lanka are close to joining them.

TNCs naturally prefer countries whose political climate is "stable", which does not necessarily coincide with strong democratic conditions. The prime minister of Singapore, a virtual TNC paradise, once declared freedom of speech a "dangerous idea" and the government expelled the Christian Conference of Asia because of its stance in solidarity with the downtrodden in Asia.

Benchmarks for human development

What do TNCs contribute to society? What is their effect on employment, on meeting people's basic needs, on health and environmental conditions?

Worldwide, TNCs have around 73 million people on their payrolls.[3] Moreover, they may generate additional jobs when they purchase goods and services from local suppliers or work with sub-contractors. However, these indirect employment effects can be negative when TNCs displace jobs from national firms. For example, Unilever's appearance in Kenya destroyed the local soap industry, because its mechanized production needs fewer workers than the labour-intensive way in which local producers made soap. The net effect on employment was thus negative.

It is estimated that TNC activity accounts for 5 percent of world employment. But this figure is small compared to the 33 percent of the globe's productive assets which they control. Because TNCs tend to be concentrated in higher-skill sectors, they usually provide higher wages, safer work conditions and better benefit packages than do local firms. This may not, however, be the case when they work through sub-contractors.[4]

A growing number of TNCs separate the physical production of goods from research and development and marketing. Nike is a prominent example. Its 9000 employees are involved in design, product development, marketing and administration, while all of its production is performed by a global network of independent sub-contractors with some 75,000 employees, most of them in low-wage countries like Indonesia. A pair of Nike athletic shoes selling for between $45 and $80 costs $5.60 to produce in Indonesia. The starting wage for the Indonesian girls and young women who sew them is $1.35 a day. Basketball star Michael Jordan's reported $20 million fee for promoting Nikes in 1992 exceeded the entire annual payroll of the Indonesian factories which make shoes. If labour costs increase, TNCs may shift production to countries where the wages are even lower. In the past five years, Nike has closed down some 20 production sites in South Korea and Taiwan, and opened new ones in China, Indonesia and Thailand where wages are rock bottom.[5]

While many people benefit from many of the products provided by TNCs, many others are largely irrelevant for the basic needs of most people in the world, and some are even dangerous. TNCs may sell pharmaceuticals or pesticides in the South which are banned in their home country. In the mid-1970s, 35 Californian workers making a pesticide to combat worms that attack banana plants, marketed under the trade names Nemagon and Fumazone, were found to be sterile. In 1977 the US Environmental Protection Agency severely restricted its use and banned it completely in 1979. Yet Dow Chemical and Shell Oil went on producing the chemical, and it continued to be shipped – without health warnings – for use in banana plantations in Central America and the Philippines.[6]

The consumer boycott of Nestlé products in the 1980s because the company marketed and distributed infant formula in the South in ways that violated the World Health Organization's 1981 International Code of Marketing of Breast Milk Substitutes is well-known. The World Council of Churches held discussions with Nestlé and changed its investment guidelines to avoid shares of Nestlé. Although these actions seemed to have had some success, new research published in January 1997 revealed that major infant-formula-producing companies were still in breach of the WHO Code.

Some TNCs have also been responsible for environmental problems. About half of the so-called greenhouse gas emissions – which lead to accelerated climate change – are generated by TNCs.[7] Commercial logging and mining by some TNCs contribute to deforestation. One of the worst industrial disasters in history occurred in the Union Carbide plant in Bhopal, India, in December 1984, when more than 40 tons of poisonous gas leaked from a negligently maintained facility, killing thousands of people and injuring many more.[8] When the oil tanker *Exxon Valdez* crashed off the coast of Alaska, thousands of gallons of oil were spilled into the ocean, with disastrous effects on marine life. Obviously, health and safety standards may also be violated by national companies, but it should be expected that TNCs, which overwhelmingly originate in the North, where they must comply with strict regulations in these areas, would apply similar standards in other countries.

While it is true that TNC activities transfer technology and management skills, the effect of this can be positive or negative. Much depends on whether or not the technology is adapted to local circumstances. The capital-intensive technologies often used by TNCs are in fact inappropriate for many countries in the South, which would benefit more from labour-intensive technologies. And if patent protection enables the ownership of the technologies to remain in the hands of the TNCs, the possibility of positive effects from technology transfer are further reduced.

Countries which host TNCs can often benefit from the substantial tax revenues. At the same time, it is not uncommon for TNCs successfully to evade paying taxes. In 1995, for example, Deutsche Bank had the second-best result in its history, with a profit of DM4.2 billion; yet its tax bill was DM377 million less than in the previous year. Also in 1995, the German giant Siemens managed by skilful calculations to pay no tax at all in its home country.[9]

One of the mechanisms used to reduce taxes is transfer pricing. As much as one-third of the world trade in goods and services now consists of transactions taking place within an individual TNC. The prices used for such transactions – the internal transfer prices – do not necessarily reflect market prices. Rather, TNCs can manipulate these prices to increase their profits and to let these profits emerge where they want. For example, the Dutch TNC Philips produced electronic components in its affiliate in northeast Brazil. On paper, these components were exported to the Netherlands for $1.00 a piece. Again on paper, Philips do Brazil in Sao Paulo bought the components from Philips in the Netherlands for $12.00 a piece. All the while the goods never left Brazil. The very low export price and the very high import price created a loss in Brazil – and a profit in the books of the head office in the Netherlands. On top of this, the Philips affiliate in the northeast of Brazil already benefited from special treatment by the government because it was supposedly contributing to the development of the poorest area of Brazil by producing export products. The Brazilian economy suffered three times: special advantages were given for exports which are not real, valuable foreign exchange currency was used to import over-priced goods, and taxes were evaded. Enormous secrecy surrounds the way in which internal transfer prices are established and used. Even governments often regard such matters as internal to the TNC. And when tax and customs investigations uncover abuses, they are frequently not publicized, and most such cases are settled out-of-court.[10]

Culture

With most TNCs originating in the North, as we have seen, the nature of the consumer goods they produce is based on Northern-style patterns of consumption. In the globalization process, TNCs are important vehicles in spreading these patterns all around the world. Some indeed see these activities as a kind of mission. Writing in the company's in-house magazine, the chairman of Philips' board of directors cited what historian Arnold Toynbee said about developments in the direction of a culture embracing the whole of humanity, through which – as the means of communication and information are perfected – all of humankind would grow to unity. According to this corporate executive, such a vision of the world is worth believing in, and Philips could make a significant contribution by focusing its intentions on this goal.[11]

Often, TNCs market consumer products by identifying them with cultural images and values drawn from Western Europe and North America. Nestlé claimed in an advertisement used in Zambia that "Nescafé makes men stronger, women more beautiful and children more intelligent". Elsewhere in Africa, visitors were greeted by a sign reading "Welcome to Nigeria, where babies are happy and healthy." The advertiser, not surprisingly, was a baby-food manufacturer.

Political effects and corporate ethics

While accounts of corruption, bribery of public officials and heavy-handed intervention – such as the role played by ITT in bringing down the Allende government in Chile in the 1970s – are well-known, most political activities by TNCs are more subtle. According to the Berlin-based anti-corruption organization Transparency International, many TNCs pay huge "consultancy fees", so that when trouble comes they can claim not to have had any idea that their "consultants" were using this money as a slush fund to bribe public officials. TNCs in Brazil spent US$2 million campaigning openly to make the new constitution favourable for foreign companies. They also joined national businesses in objecting to clauses favourable to workers.[12] A United Nations report has observed:

> The mere presence and operation of a TNC affiliate may have significant effects on the host country's political situation. The establishment of business connections and alliances may lead to effective support for, or the strengthening of, various domestic interest groups and may thereby affect the host country's political life.[13]

During the 1970s and 1980s the political effects of TNC activities were the object of campaigns against their presence in Rhodesia (now Zimbabwe) and South Africa. Through their activities in these countries, TNCs strengthened the position of racist regimes. The WCC, its member churches and many ecumenical organizations were active in efforts aimed at the withdrawal of foreign investment from these countries and the end of bank loans to the apartheid regime in South Africa.[14] Considerable attention focused on the record of Shell in this respect. In one discussion with critical church officials, the president of Shell became so annoyed that he remarked: "You may be the prophets but we are the kings!" More recently, Shell has come under international criticism because of massive pollution in Nigeria's Ogoniland and for failing to use its influence to try to prevent the execution of Ogoni human rights activists who had criticized the oil industry for its environmental record.[15] The general business principles which Shell adopted in 1997 may help to improve the company's policies and they can be used as an instrument for civil society to hold Shell accountable to its stated principles.

The policies of TNCs have always been monitored carefully and critically by organized labour and its political allies. In the 1970s, however, consumer organizations and other civil society groups also began to challenge TNCs on ethical issues. The initial response of many TNCs was often crude and cynical – basically that their main task was to make profits and that it was up to others, like governments, to take care of the side effects of their activities. Companies are first and foremost responsible to the shareholders who have invested in them, and corporate responsibility ends at the company's gate. Church-related groups questioning Philips about its activities in South Africa were dismissed as "Christian agitators" by the chairman of the board. A spokesperson for Shell Norway, asked whether the company had any scruples about selling petroleum products to the South African military and police, retorted that "from the fact that Hitler ate pumpernickel, it does not necessarily follow that there is anything wrong with pumpernickel". The same company defended its presence in apartheid South Africa by saying that if it left some other company would take over its place – an argument which Archbishop Desmond Tutu once observed is on the same ethical level as saying, "If I don't rape your wife, somebody else will."

Over time, the level of ethical discourse has improved. Corporate executives today are likely to be able to see the difference between baking pumpernickel and supplying oil to an oppressive regime. Nevertheless, the mentality of the top management and the corporate culture may differ from company to company. Some have developed a more open ear and a better antenna for responsible corporate citizenship in today's world. Companies which produce consumer products have extra reasons to be sensitive to criticism since they are vulnerable to consumer actions.

Obviously, if its activities are not profitable a corporation will cease to exist. But there is a growing recognition that this argument cannot be used to justify engaging in any activity whatever in any way whatever. Even that which is legally permitted is not always ethically desirable. Corporate responsibility is more than providing the highest possible financial return for shareholders and other investors. The interest of other "stakeholders" – employees, customers, suppliers and communities – must also be taken into account.

Some companies have even hired ethicists and theologians to help them address these issues.[16]

Codes of conduct

Many companies today, including Shell, have high-minded internal mission statements and codes of conduct. Some have endorsed agreements such as the Business Charter for Sustainable Development of the International Chamber of Commerce. Other companies have established codes of conduct for their sub-contractors. The Levi Strauss code sets environmental, ethical, health and safety standards, and prohibits child labour, prison labour and discrimination. It requires that sub-contractors pay the minimum wage and employ workers at most 60 hours per week with one day off.[17] Some may be tempted to dismiss all this as a public relations exercise, but citizens' movements and NGOs can use the codes as instruments to improve corporate responsibility.

Of the international codes of conduct for TNCs, the best known are the Guidelines for Multinational Enterprises of the Organization for Economic Cooperation and Development and the Tripartite Declaration of Principles Concerning Multinational Enterprises and Social Policy of the International Labour Organization. The OECD Guidelines apply only to the few industrialized countries that are signatories and the ILO Declaration focuses mainly on social policies. Business drew up its own code through the Guidelines for International Investments of the International Chamber of Commerce.

Efforts to formulate a more comprehensive and globally applicable code of conduct began in the early 1970s when the United Nations established the Commission on Transnational Corporations. Several drafts were produced but over time the political will to adopt a code has waned. In 1992, the president of the UN general assembly, Samir Shihabi, reported that no consensus was possible on the draft code: "Delegations felt that the changed international economic environment and the importance attached to encouraging foreign investment required a fresh approach." It was suggested that this "fresh approach" take the form of guidelines for ethical business practices, but it is unlikely that guidelines would have the same impact as an international code.

The history of the UN code of conduct reflects the trend towards greater liberalization. Some Southern countries which were previously critical of TNCs have adopted a more conciliatory tone.[18] Governments in the South now queue up to attract TNCs, competing with each other's offers of tax breaks and other incentives to lure foreign companies while taking for granted the possible negative consequences. When the UN Commission on TNCs was terminated, some of its activities were taken up by the UN Conference on Trade and Development (UNCTAD). The earlier valuable studies on TNCs have largely been replaced by UNCTAD materials advising governments how best to lure TNCs to their country. Southern governments and TNCs now seem to live in peace with each other. Time will tell whether this is peace by conviction or peace by surrender.

Churches and TNCs

The activities of TNCs have not escaped the attention of the churches. As early as 1937, the Oxford conference of the Life and Work movement on "Church, Community and State" noted that "the earlier stage of competitive capitalism has been gradually replaced by a monopolistic stage, and this economic change has brought with it corresponding political consequences". The original ideal of modern democracy was becoming increasingly difficult to achieve, since "centres of economic power have been formed which are not responsible to any organ of the community and which in practice constitute something in the nature of a tyranny over the lives of masses of men".

In 1955, the WCC Central Committee pointed to the need for critical study and evaluation of the impact of private trade and enterprise in the world's "economically under-developed nations". During the following 20 years, concern about the activities of TNCs increased, leading the WCC's Nairobi assembly in 1975 to recommend that a special study programme on TNCs be initiated. This programme was carried out between 1978 and 1982 under the energetic leadership of the Brazilian economist Marcos Arruda. The programme was not neutral: the WCC Executive Committee, meeting in Zurich in 1978, had specified that it should be undertaken from a perspective of solidarity with victims of TNC operations.[19]

An important role in this discussion has been played by the Interfaith Centre on Corporate Responsibility (ICCR), which is related to the US National Council of Churches. ICCR is a coalition of 275 Protestant, Roman Catholic and Jewish communities and judicatories, agencies, pension funds and health care systems. In 1996, these organizations initiated 185 resolutions on corporate policies related to social justice, military production and the environment with 126 companies. The model of ICCR has been followed elsewhere, notably the Netherlands and the United Kingdom, and in many countries ecumenical organizations are engaged in reflection and action concerning economic issues and activities of TNCs.

The recognition is growing that stereotyped views of TNCs are not helpful and that national corporations may behave as well or as badly as their transnational counterparts. There are many people – church members and others – who work in the corporate world and struggle with their consciences over reconciling their convictions with the work they have to do. One may hope that those within the corporate world and outside of it recognize that many corporate activities do have beneficial effects, but that it is always necessary carefully to discern their effects on different groups in society.

NOTES

[1] Cf. *World Investment Report 1996: Investment, Trade and International Policy Arrangements*, New York and Geneva, United Nations, 1996, pp.3,16.

50

2 Cf. Eric Kolodner, *Transnational Corporations: Impediments or Catalysts of Social Development?*, Geneva, UN Research Institute for Social Development, 1994.

3 Cf. *Transnationals* (UNCTAD), Vol. 6, no.3, Oct.-Dec. 1994.

4 Cf. Richard J. Barnet and John Cavanagh, *Global Dreams: Imperial Corporations and the New World Order*, New York, Simon & Schuster, 1994, pp.331ff.

5 Cf. *Terre Nouvelle*, March 1997; Richard J. Barnet and John Cavanagh, "Just Undo It: Nike's Exploited Workers", *The New York Times*, 3 Feb. 1994.

6 On pesticides, see Kolodner, *op. cit.*, p.8; David Weir and Marc Schapiro, *Circle of Poison: Pesticides and People in a Hungry World*, San Francisco, Institute for Food and Development Policy, 1981, p.11; *The Economist*, 12 March 1994.

7 *Climate Change and Transnational Corporations*, New York, United Nations, 1992, p.2.

8 On the Bhopal tragedy, see the report *Asia's Struggle to Affirm Wholeness of Life*, Hong Kong, Christian Conference of Asia, 1985.

9 Cf. Hans Küng, *A Global Ethic for Global Politics and Economics*, London, SCM Press, 1997, p.164.

10 Cf. *NRC*, 12 Dec. 1978; *Transnational Corporations and Transfer Prices: A Delicate Example from Brazil*, Amsterdam, OSACI, 1981.

11 *Philips Koerier*, 11 Jan. 1979.

12 *Multinational Monitor*, July-Aug. 1988.

13 *Transnational Corporations in World Development*, New York, United Nations, 1978, p.75.

14 See *The World Council of Churches and Bank Loans to South Africa*, Geneva, WCC, 1977; Barbara Rogers, *Race: No Peace Without Justice*, Geneva, WCC, 1980.

15 *Ogoni: The Struggle Continues*, Geneva, WCC, 1996.

16 Cf. Urs P. Gasche, *The "Strategies" of the Multinationals Up Against Their Critics*, Berne Declaration, 1975.

17 Kolodner, *op. cit.*, p.25.

18 Cf. Patrick A. Muma, "TNCs and Economic Development", *CTC Reporter* (UN), no. 31, spring 1991.

19 For a report see *Churches and the Transnational Corporation: An Ecumenical Programme*, Geneva, WCC, 1983.

5. International Finance

The Bretton Woods Conference

The International Monetary Fund (IMF) and the World Bank were conceived when the second world war was still raging. Adolf Hitler's vision of a "New Order" for the post-war world induced both Britain and the USA to reflect on their own plans. Proposals by both the eminent British economist John Maynard Keynes and Dexter White, an advisor to the US Secretary of the Treasury, were published in April 1942. In July 1944 delegations from 44 nations came together at the resort of Bretton Woods in New Hampshire. Over four weeks they thrashed out the post-war international economic system. Their goals were to make post-war reconstruction easier and to foster the economic integration of the world through trade and stable monetary policies.

The negotiations in Bretton Woods showed the leading role being assumed by the US. Keynes may have been a more subtle economic thinker, but White had the more powerful government behind him, and on many important issues the US got its way. Keynes wanted the IMF and the World Bank to be located in London as the centre of international trade, or else in New York (seat of the United Nations), but the USA insisted on Washington. The tradition was established that the head of the IMF would always be a European while the head of the World Bank would be from the USA.

The Soviet Union sent delegates to Bretton Woods. India and Latin American countries were also present, but most other Southern countries were still colonies and not represented. After their independence nearly all joined the IMF – a requirement for obtaining loans from the World Bank. By the time the US Congress ratified the Bretton Woods agreements in July 1945 the first signs of the cold war were already emerging; and after the Soviet Union had been refused a US loan, it was clear that it would not join the Bretton Woods institutions. Instead, it established its own bloc, the COMECON.

The initial structure envisaged at Bretton Woods rested on four pillars: an International Bank for Reconstruction and Development (popularly known as the World Bank), the IMF, the International Trade Organization (ITO) and the

United Nations. But despite a fully negotiated agreement for an ITO in 1947, this never came into existence, blocked by fears in the US Congress that it would harm US interests. It was replaced by the General Agreement on Tariffs and Trade (GATT), which was essentially a framework for successive rounds of negotiations and lacked the jurisdiction and continuity of a permanent institution. Nor did GATT touch what the Bretton Woods Conference had seen as a key issue: stabilization of commodity prices. To fill the gap, the United Nations Conference on Trade and Development (UNCTAD) was established in 1964. But the powerful Western nations largely ignored UNCTAD, and its activities were mainly limited to studies. As part of the UN system, UNCTAD decisions are made by the "one nation, one vote" system, giving preponderance to the South, whereas the Bretton Woods institutions operate on a voting system which benefits rich countries. The US, for example, controls 17.2 percent of the voting stock while 45 African countries together only have 4 percent of the total. But while the recently established World Trade Organization (WTO) does operate on the "one country, one vote" system, Southern countries still feel marginalized because they cannot muster the expertise and number of qualified officials to form an effective force in the WTO.

When the UN Charter was approved in 1945, the World Bank and the IMF formally became specialized agencies in the UN system. The UN itself was supposed to be the focus for global economic management through its General Assembly and the Economic and Social Council (ECOSOC). But it has never been able to play this role, because the rich countries have preferred to work through the IMF and the World Bank, where their influence was much greater. A further step away from multilateralism was the organization by the most powerful Northern countries of the Group of Seven (G-7), in which important decisions about economic coordination are taken by governments representing only 12 percent of the world's population.

The IMF was established to promote international cooperation on monetary policies, exchange rate stability and the expansion of world trade. A country with a short-term balance of payments problem could turn to the IMF for help rather than curtailing imports, devaluating its currency or imposing exchange rate controls which would distort international trade. From the very beginning it was clear that the "free trade" which the Bretton Woods system aimed to promote gave the rich countries a powerful role, from which they drew considerable benefits. For example, the IMF financed 10 percent of the US deficit from 1960 to 1967 even if this meant that its rules had to be bent. By investing its own sizeable funds in US government securities, it increased its loans to the US even further.[1]

The World Bank was set up to provide capital for reconstruction and development. After the war-torn countries had rebuilt their economies, it turned its attention to the South. Assuming that development could be achieved by transferring money to the South, the World Bank saw itself as an intermediary, borrowing money on Northern capital markets to lend to countries in the South, not forgetting that it should make a profit on these operations. When it was realized that the success or failure of the projects and programmes to which it made loans depended to a large extent on government policies, the conditions for lending were broadened to include national economic and financial policies.

Measured by reconstruction and the expansion of world trade, the Bretton Woods arrangements were a great success. In the two decades after 1945, the ruined economies of Europe and Japan grew faster than ever before or since, achieving living standards broadly comparable with those in the United States. Between 1948 and 1971, world industrial production (in real terms) grew by 5.6 percent each year. Trade expanded even faster, thereby promoting international economic integration. These two decades were a time without parallel in the economic history of the world. Unequal as the distribution of the benefits was – both nationally and internationally – it was significantly less unfavourable to poor people and poor countries than the ensuing period has been.

The cornerstone of the Bretton Woods system was a regime of fixed exchange rates. The prices of currencies were expressed in gold or in US dollars, which could be exchanged at a fixed price into gold. Adjustments were allowed only in exceptional circumstances and under IMF's supervision. The first cracks in the Bretton Woods system appeared in the early 1960s when the number of US dollars circulating in the world economy soared as a result of the continuing US balance of payments deficits. Out of fear of a devaluation of the dollar, many of these dollars were cashed in for gold, which started to pour out of the US. The situation worsened in the late 1960s, when the high costs of the war in Vietnam led to rising inflation and ever-bigger US deficits. Faced with a choice between a devaluation of the dollar and the politically unpopular step of inducing an economic slow-down, President Richard Nixon chose the former and suspended the dollar's link to gold in 1973. The Bretton Woods system came to an end, and the world's big economies shifted to the regime of freely floating exchange rates that continues to this day. One of the results was that currency speculators appeared on the scene again and control over international money and capital flows greatly diminished.

The fundamental changes in the international monetary system required a rethinking of the role of the two pillars of the now-defunct Bretton Woods system, the IMF and the World Bank. The IMF's role of supervising the system of fixed exchange rates no longer mattered, and its mandate to supply short-term credit to countries suffering balance of payments difficulties took on a quite different character. The IMF soon assumed a new job by focusing on providing finances to countries in distress – first those in the South as a result of the debt crisis, and then in Eastern Europe and the former Soviet Union after the collapse of the centrally planned economies in 1989. Once Western Europe was rebuilt, the World Bank also turned its attention to the South. With the debt crisis, the Bank moved into the area of policy reform and structural adjustment lending. It greatly increased its lending for macro-economic and sectoral programmes rather than for specific projects. Both the IMF and the World Bank began to insist that receiving countries should adopt certain macro-economic policies as a condition for their loans. Such conditionality became the most severely criticized aspect of their work.

The debt crisis

African governments annually pay more than US$13 billion to their Northern creditors, more than double what they spend on health and primary education combined. Uganda spends around $2.50 per person per year on health compared to $30 on debt servicing. In Nicaragua, debt repayments account for more than a third of government spending, double the amount spent for education and clean water provision. In 1994, Zambia spent thirty times more on debt repayments than it did on education. The World Bank's own poverty studies say that "serious drops in attendance rates have been observed, disproportionately affecting girls". Between 1983 and 1994, Africa as a region paid almost $5 billion more to the IMF than it received.[2]

Facts like these are usually referred to as the debt crisis. Its origins can be described briefly. As we have seen, the persistent US deficits in the 1960s led to large quantities of dollars circulating outside the US. These quantities increased further when the oil-producing countries sharply raised prices in 1973 and stacked away their growing revenues in Western banks. Seeking markets for these huge amounts of dollars, Western banks decided to lend to Southern governments. They saw these loans as relatively low-risk transactions, believing that countries would not go bankrupt. For Southern countries in turn, the loans constituted an attractive source of funding, especially because the interest rates were low.

This situation came to an end with the second major hike in oil prices in 1979-1980, which caused serious problems for non-oil producing Southern countries. Moreover, the US increased its interest rates, dramatically raising the cost of servicing the loans. The recession in the industrialized world in the 1970s depressed the volume and prices of exports from Southern countries, making things even worse. The real prices of commodities, on which many Southern countries still heavily depend, were 45 percent lower in the 1990s than in the 1980s – and 10 percent below the lowest level during the Great Depression.[3] An acute crisis emerged in August 1982 when Mexico announced that it could no longer afford to meet its repayment obligations. The threat that this would lead to the collapse of US banks and, through a chain reaction, of the whole international monetary system led to very quick steps to provide extra funds for Mexico. Since 1982, emergency measures have prevented the collapse of the international monetary system, but the root causes have never been addressed.

Besides loans provided by commercial banks, bilateral (when countries receive credits from governments, mainly in the North) and multilateral debt (resulting from loans of the IMF, the World Bank and regional development banks) also increased. Over time, transnational banks built up their reserves, allowing them to write off major parts of their bad debts in Southern countries. Bilateral debt and in some instances multilateral debt now constitute the major problems for many Southern countries.

Conditionality and adjustment

There is nothing wrong with debt as such if you stand a chance of paying back the loan. Nor is it illegitimate for a lender to attach certain just and reasonable conditions to a loan. And not many people would question the need for those who are indebted to make adjustments when circumstances require this. Yet debt, "conditionality" and "adjustment" have become subjects of considerable debate and controversy in the world today. Why is this so?

The source of the debate is the fact that a number of Southern countries are finding it impossible to service, let alone pay back the loans they contracted some 20 years ago. Besides the external factors mentioned above, there are also internal reasons for this: the money may have been used for unproductive or prestige projects to glorify the ruling class, or for military expenditures, or for the personal enrichment of corrupt leaders. In some cases national disasters such as prolonged droughts have prevented countries from generating enough money to repay the loans. Many have thus contracted new loans to service the old debts, creating an even higher foreign debt. The spiral of these events caused the "debt trap".

Of the 54 countries which the World Bank classifies as "low-income" (annual income of less than US$695 per person), 32 are reckoned to have a severe debt problem. Together with a handful of heavily indebted but marginally richer countries, they form the core of the poor-country debt crisis. Almost all are in Africa; and although their combined debt is only 15 percent of the total external debts of Southern countries, it is huge in comparison with the size of their economies. Guinea-Bissau, with a population of 1 million, is in the worst situation. The value of its outstanding debts is more than 11 times that of its annual exports (mainly cashew nuts). As a rule of thumb, any country with outstanding debts of more than double the value of its exports is in trouble. Although not all countries are in as bad a situation as Guinea-Bissau, it is obvious that the "low-income" countries as a group are truly bankrupt. Clearly, there can be something wrong with debts.

Can something also be wrong with adjustment and conditionality? The debate on this question centres on what the goals are, which criteria should be used, who sets them and whether they should be uniform or allow for flexibility. Typically, the IMF's Structural Adjustment Programmes (SAPs) insist on the devaluation of a country's currency to promote exports, an increase in interest rates to promote domestic savings, cuts in the national budget, privatization of state enterprises and liberalization of the economy. There are several problems with this approach.

First, if many Southern debtor countries devalue their currencies to promote their exports at more or less the same time, the result is likely to be lower export prices and decreased revenues, benefiting only those who import the products. Food security may also be affected if the effort to promote exports leads to a shift from food crops like beans and maize to export crops like coffee and cacao.

Second, cuts in government bureaucracies can lead to increased unemployment. For example, only 95,000 of Mozambique's 7 million adults are formally employed. Structural adjustment has not contributed to a solution for this problem; on the contrary, it has cost 30,000 jobs.[4]

Cuts in government budgets often hurt the poor the most, since the areas affected almost always include government spending on health, education, transport and food subsidies. Naturally, this provokes popular reactions, such as those which followed the implementation of SAPs in Egypt, Jamaica, Sudan and Turkey. Bitter Senegalese stormed through the streets of Dakar when the price of imported rice, sugar and cooking oil doubled following the devaluation of their currency, the CFA franc. Angry Zimbabweans rioted when their government ended bread subsidies. Many more examples could be mentioned.

It is too easy to blame this only on the IMF. Although the chance of dying from malnutrition or preventable disease in poor countries is 33 times greater than the chances of dying in a war with their neighbours, poor countries have, on average, about 20 soldiers for every doctor. Many of the countries which are the keenest on military spending are among the world's poorest, and often the armies thus built up are unleashed on their own populations. Between 1960 and 1987, according to the UN Development Programme, military spending in poor countries increased three times as fast as in rich ones. South Asia and Sub-Saharan Africa, where 800 million people live in absolute poverty, have increased their annual arms spending to US$19 billion and $8 billion respectively, much of it going to Northern countries. This is not to say that defence spending is never justified, but if highly indebted countries must reduce government spending, should they not consider reducing military expenditures before cutting social services? Nothing in the SAP recipes prevents them from doing this.

A third difficulty with SAPs is that while privatization of state enterprises may be a good idea from an economic point of view, it often leads to higher unemployment, especially in urban areas.

Are SAPs successful measured by their own goals? A World Bank study of Sub-Saharan Africa showed that in no single country did adjustment programmes work unambiguously in the right way. The best that can be said of Africa's most faithful implementers of SAPs is that things are no longer getting worse. Restored growth was rarely achieved in practice, and where adjustment policies reduced deficits it was often at the cost of inducing recession. In short, the UN Development Programme concludes, they often balanced budgets by un-balancing people's lives.

Of course, it can be argued that countries have failed to implement fully the "advice" of the IMF and World Bank. But there is also a problem with the rigidity the IMF displays in its analysis, selection of targets, strategy of adjustment, time frameworks imposed and fairly uniform prescriptions given to different countries. The World Bank, which unlike the IMF is a development agency, is more pragmatic, but it also adheres to two questionable ideological perspectives: the virtual equation of economic growth with development and the belief that under almost any circumstances market forces are the best instrument to resolve political-economic problems – including meeting basic needs and eradicating absolute poverty. Some well-known critics of the World Bank have commented that "this supranational, non-democratic institution functions very much like the church, in fact the mediaeval church. It has a doctrine, a rigidly structured hierarchy preaching and imposing this doctrine and a quasi-religious mode of self-justification." Others have spoken about a "fundamentalist theology" which reigns in the World Bank.[5]

Because SAPs have not produced their stated objectives but are still prescribed as the only available medicine, and because they primarily hurt those who are already suffering and who bear no responsibility whatever for the debt crisis, it is clear that the challenge here is not only economic but also ethical. A WCC report puts it this way:

> Ultimately many choices and decisions in respect to how to adjust, over what time frame and with what balance of instruments and targets rest on value judgments. If demand is to be cut, whose access to resources is to be curtailed? That of the military? Of domestic elites? Of external creditors? Or of poor workers and peasants? If supply is to be enhanced, supply of what and for whom – of food, water, health and education for the poor? Of luxury consumer goods for elites? Of basic consumption and investment goods for local use? Of amenity products for local elites or, via export, for financing amenity imports?
>
> A commitment to the poor cannot usually be articulated effectively by opposing adjustment, but only through informing choices in respect to adjustment and especially as to who bears costs and receives benefits. The answers from the point of view of that commitment, which is ultimately one of values and of ideology, do differ from those consistent with commitments to maximize production as an overriding end in and of itself, to maximize national military capacity or to stabilize and expand the power and perquisites of existing dominant elites.[6]

Proposals for debt reduction

Many proposals have been put forward to tackle the various forms of foreign debt. One of the first was the Baker Plan of 1985, which sought to enable countries which owed large amounts to private commercial banks to "grow out of their debts" by a combination of vigorous economic reforms and the provision of new funds by banks and other organizations, notably the IMF and the World Bank. The results were disappointing, largely because of the reluctance of banks to lend any more money.

In the meantime, a "second-hand market" for debt emerged. Creditors started to sell their claims on debtors at a discount to others. These "debt swaps" presented debtors with an opportunity to reduce their foreign debt, and formed the basis of the Brady Plan of 1989. Its central idea was that debtor countries willing to engage in economic reform would receive funds from the IMF, the World Bank and donor countries with which they could buy their own debts at the reduced second-hand market price. Although the success of this scheme was limited, several countries were able to use it to reduce their commercial debts.

A number of initiatives have been taken by Northern governments to cancel, reduce or reschedule bilateral debt.[7] In 1994 the "Paris Club" of creditor countries agreed in principle to reduce by two-thirds the outstanding debt of the poorest countries (as long as they were reforming their economies under IMF surveillance). In 1996, this was increased to 80 percent. But the effects of this are not as dramatic as it sounds, because not all outstanding debts are included.

Lately, the issue of multilateral debt has attracted much attention. For example, two-thirds of the foreign debt of Uganda and Ghana and almost three-quarters of Burkina Faso's debt is owed to international institutions. For some countries, multilateral debt service payments represent 50 percent of the total debt service. The longtime refusal of the IMF and the World Bank to recognize multilateral debt as a problem became untenable after the 1995 World Summit for Social Development called on the two institutions "to seek a durable solution to this increasing problem". One factor which may have caused a change of heart is growing resentment among creditor countries that the World Bank and the IMF are "preferred creditors", which must be paid back before other creditors are paid. Therefore, these institutions are often seen as the true beneficiaries of bilateral debt reduction.

The World Bank and the IMF have three worries: that relieving debt sets a bad example, that it could damage their own standing and creditworthiness and that it might deprive worthier borrowers of loans they deserve. Of these objections, the first is the least convincing. The risk of setting a precedent by writing off a debt can be minimized by being more selective in the future. Besides, it should be recognized that some of the World Bank's loans are bad examples in themselves.

While there is more weight to the argument that debt relief would harm the lending organization's own financial health and credibility, the IMF, with gold stocks worth about $40 billion, has little to worry about. The World Bank might have a greater problem, since it borrows on international capital markets. If the markets would see debt relief as a weakening of the Bank's balance sheet, it could be forced to borrow at higher costs. But since the World Bank also has considerable reserves and is backed by Northern governments, these risks are again low.

To the third worry – that money spent on debt relief would deprive others of loans – there is no real answer except that the sale of a portion of the IMF's gold stock could provide new and extra resources.

In September 1996, the Highly Indebted Poor Countries (HIPC) Initiative was accepted to help reduce to sustainable levels the foreign debt of countries whose total debt exceeds 200-250 percent of their total exports, whose costs for servicing the debt (interest plus principal due) exceed 20-25 percent of their export earnings, and who are vulnerable in other ways (such as being dependent on a small range of export products). The breakthrough of the plan – which is reckoned to cost between $5.5 and 7.7 billion – is that it is comprehensive, covering commercial, bilateral and multilateral debt. For the first time, multilateral creditors will reduce debt, not just reschedule it. Another groundbreaking aspect is that a commitment by the debtor government to reducing poverty is used as a criterion for eligibility.

Although accepted, it is not yet clear how the HIPC Initiative is to be financed. Germany, Italy and Switzerland have opposed the sale of part of the IMF's gold stock for this purpose, arguing that such a sale would set a precedent. Such an argument is difficult to understand. In the international monetary system, gold is a relic of the past and is not productive when it simply sits in the vaults of the IMF or any other financial organization. If it is sold, the proceeds could be invested, keeping the value of the IMF resources intact, while the return on investment could be used for debt relief.

Although many have welcomed the HIPC Initiative in principle, it has also been criticized because it is built on standard conditionality, and the qualifications required for debt relief are so tough that very few countries will be able to meet them.

Reviewing the international financial system

The IMF and the World Bank are now more than 50 years old. Any institution of that age needs a critical assessment of whether the goals for which it was established are still valid and what a changed environment may mean for its functioning. We have seen that both institutions have shown some flexibility in adapting to new circumstances: the World Bank by turning towards the South after postwar reconstruction in Europe, the IMF by providing loans to debtor countries – under strict conditionality – after the emergence of the debt crisis in the early 1980s. Nevertheless, there is a need to question the role and functioning of both institutions in light of the changed situation in the world and growing globalization which has revolutionized international finance.

The vision of Bretton Woods was based on two premises: (1) that the most significant actor in the international order is the sovereign state; and (2) that except for the United Nations, which has general powers, each international organization should have a limited mandate to deal with a specific and defined set of problems. This situation has changed substantially. The structure of international organizations based on exclusive state membership is being challenged by the increasing number of actors on the international scene, not only TNCs but also nongovernmental organizations. At the same time, the sovereignty of states has declined in the sense that they have a diminished ability to manage problems within their borders. Most problems can be addressed effectively only through collaborative efforts involving states, the (international) civil society and international institutions. The World Bank has developed some links with civil society, but international organizations have in general failed to respond adequately to these new challenges. The result is that most of them are seeking to solve current problems with institutional arrangements designed for a bygone era.[8]

Several other important issues call for a re-conceptualization of the type of global monetary system most appropriate for today's world.

First is the absence of an independent reserve currency. At present, the US dollar functions as a currency accepted almost everywhere in the world. This gives considerable advantages to the United States. As Dutch economist Bob Goudzwaard points out, the United States can simply print, at hardly any cost, what must be borrowed at high costs by poor countries. As long as US dollars continue to be accepted almost universally, this will not create any problems for the US. For the South, however, the creation of this type of money leads to de-development. If there were any element of justice in how money is created in this world, according to Goudzwaard, the debt crisis could have been avoided.[9] Replacing the US dollar with a neutral reserve currency could therefore introduce more equity into the relations between poorer and richer countries. An effort to that end was made in 1968 when the IMF agreed to issue an artificial reserve currency named the Special Drawing Right (SDR). These SDRs could be used for international transactions among nations, and between nations and a number of official multilateral financial institutions. The creation and distribution of SDRs could be linked to need rather than, as is the case now, to currencies like the US dollar, Japanese yen and German mark, at the will of individual nations.

Second, there is no mechanism and no capacity to control the excessive volatility of foreign exchange markets which has resulted from economic liberalization policies. Daily turnover on these markets has grown to around $1.3 trillion – about the same as the total currency reserves of the world's central banks. Most of these transactions are speculative.

Two striking demonstrations of central bankers' inability to withstand speculative onslaughts have been the bursting of the European monetary system's exchange-rate mechanism in 1992 and the collapse of the Mexican peso in December

1994. In the light of such episodes, some policy makers and economists are now arguing for the taming of the foreign-exchange market. One proposal for cooling international speculation is to levy a relatively small tax (on the order of 0.1 percent) on all international financial transactions (known as the "Tobin Tax" after its originator, Nobel prize-winning economist James Tobin – though a similar idea was proposed by Keynes already in 1936). Such a small tax would discourage short-term speculation without interfering with long-term investments or trade. Although the idea has been dismissed as unworkable and interfering with the market, support for it has recently been mounting, not only because it would dampen speculation, but also because it would generate considerable revenues which governments and the international community could use.[10]

A third reason to take a hard look at the present international monetary system is the consistent failure of the SAPs, the main remedy applied by the dominant actors, to cure the ills for which they are prescribed. Indeed, this cure, much like mediaeval bloodletting, has left many patients even more sick than they were before. The persistence of faith in the healing power of the market forces even as the symptoms worsen is in itself a reason to review critically the assumptions behind the policies of the World Bank and the IMF. But it is also necessary to re-assess the "one size fits all" approach with which SAPs are applied to markedly different situations all over the world. The need for flexibility and adaptability was recognized at the World Summit for Social Development in 1995, where governments committed themselves to "strive to ensure that structural adjustment programmes respond to the economic and social conditions, concerns and needs of each country" and that they include social development goals, in particular eradicating poverty, promoting full and productive employment and enhancing social integration, while ensuring that women do not bear a disproportionate burden of the transitional costs of such processes. Taken seriously, these commitments could lead to a complete overhaul of SAPs.

Ideally, a new global central bank should be established in order to begin restoring global public good over national or private interest.[11] An international bank (already proposed by Keynes), could function only if member countries were prepared to yield some degree of sovereignty in the exercise of economic policy – which may at present be little more than a visionary hope. A more pragmatic attitude may be more effective. Transformation will engender less opposition than proposing major new institutions. If Reginald Green is correct in asserting that "wholesale demolition to produce a *tabula rasa* is a concept not easily transformed into political process",[12] it may be more fruitful to concentrate on proposals to reform the Bretton Woods institutions rather than on those which aim to abolish or replace them.

Reforming the Bretton Woods institutions

Proposals to reform the Bretton Woods institutions have focused on the following issues:

1. *Equitable representation.* Currently, voting power in the IMF and the World Bank is based on a country's economic strength and the contributions it makes to these institutions. The logic to this linkage is that the World Bank and the IMF are lending institutions, and lender governments can be expected to demand some degree of control over the use of their funds. Nevertheless, the decision-making process would be less undemocratic if the voting system would reflect the distribution of population among nations. Furthermore, recent research by the IMF has shown that the gross national product (GNP) figures on the basis of which votes are allocated seriously underestimate the true GNP of Southern countries. A calculation based on "purchasing power parity", rather than the official exchange rates with the US dollar, corrected for currency fluctuations and different costs of living, would be more in tune with reality.

2. *Asymmetry.* The Bretton Woods system was designed to achieve balance of payments equilibria. Both countries with a deficit and countries with a surplus should work to eliminate these imbalances. Although a proposal by Keynes

to tax countries with a surplus faded into the background, it was taken for granted that the IMF would symmetrically supervise all members. In practice, however, it is common for non-borrowers entirely to ignore IMF advice. The United States is a prime example. The IMF has consistently high-lighted the negative global effects of US budget deficits, and has publicly urged Washington to reduce these, to no avail. This asymmetry is all the more objectionable since policies pursued by Northern countries like the US often have strong negative effects on the South. For many, the IMF will never be a credible institution if this asymmetry is not addressed.

3. *Accountability and transparency*. Institutions whose activities directly affect the lives of many persons must be accountable to the public. While not everything should be disclosed at every stage of a delicate negotiation process, the public has a right to know what considerations have led to decisions and to express its opinion on the issues at stake. Too much secrecy surrounds the Bretton Woods institutions. The World Bank has taken some steps to change this situa-tion by setting up a committee through which NGOs can express their opinions on its policies and an Inspection Panel to investigate complaints by those who claim to have been harmed by the Bank's failure to comply with its rules and policies. Although its powers are only advisory, its findings are publicly available. The IMF still remains largely exempt from even such limited accountability and transparency.

4. *Participation and devolution*. Directly linked to accountability and transparency are the issues of participa-tion and devolution. Serious consideration should be given to transferring responsibilities from the Bretton Woods institu-tions to regional multilateral development banks such as the Inter-American Development Bank, the African Develop-ment Bank, the Asian Development Bank and the European Bank for Reconstruction and Development. Such devolution would be a small step towards recognizing that participation in development of those most affected by it is a *sine qua non* for lasting success. Decentralization could also make poss-ible a greater diversity of approaches.[13]

Even these pragmatic proposals are likely to encounter considerable resistance. In the end, the problems are much more fundamental, reflecting a deep-seated mindset behind the present international financial disorder. The debt crisis is only the tip of the iceberg; and if all foreign debt were cancelled, there is a fair chance that it would soon reappear unless broader issues such as unequal trade relations are addressed at the same time.

The challenge is nothing less than to search for an equitable global structure of institutions, which essentially requires a new development paradigm built on justice, participation and sustainability. Churches, among others, could play an important role in promoting such a fundamental change in worldview.

Churches and the international financial system

Financial issues have often attracted the attention of churches and theologians. Initially, the focus was on usury, which once meant nothing more than lending money in return for interest. Three of the world's major religions have formal prohibitions against it, though these have not always been followed strictly. The two essential arguments against interest are that lenders are in effect getting something for nothing, and that persons should help neighbours in need without hope of gain. The view that multiplying money by charging interest is unnatural can be traced back to Aristotle, whose writings on this began an influential tradition of natural law. Jews cited the Hebrew Bible and Talmudic writings which condemned usury. Frequent reference was made to Deuteronomy 23:19-20: "You shall not charge interest on loans to another Israelite... On loans to a foreigner you may charge interest" – a text which some mediaeval Christians interpreted as a ground for exempting Jews from the prohibition against usury.

In the 8th century Pope Leo the Great forbade clergy to act as usurers and declared that laypersons who did so would be guilty of seeking *turpe lucrum* (shameful gain). Pope Alexander III in 1179 excommunicated usurers and denied them a Christian burial. A few years later, Pope Urban III cited Luke 6:35 – "lend expecting nothing in return" – as evidence that Jesus himself forbade usury. A decree of the Council of Vienna in 1311 declared any legitimation of usury to be heresy.

The theological discourse changed under the influence of the Reformation. Martin Luther said the question of interest should be settled by the princes and by individual conscience; he himself thought 8 percent legitimate. John Calvin thought usurers should be expelled from the church, but he pointed out that Israelites lived in a different political-economic situation from the present and that their laws cannot simply be transplanted to other situations. Since land and capital are interchangeable as investments, he argued, interest is as ethically justifiable as rent. No doubt Calvin's views on this were influenced by the importance of Geneva as a centre of trade, industry and finance. A Geneva church ordinance of 1541 allowed interest of 5 percent; this was raised to 6.7 percent in 1557.

Although resistance against charging excessive interest rates endures, the principle of charging interest as such is widely accepted.[14] Since inflation erodes capital, asking interest allows a lender to recover at least the real value of the loan. Both the Vatican's Bank of the Holy Spirit and the Ecumenical Church Loan Fund (ECLOF) and Ecumenical Development Co-operative Society (EDCS), related to the World Council of Churches, work with interest.

The churches' critiques of the international financial system usually begin by pointing to its effects on people. Typical is a statement by the WCC Central Committee in 1985: "The basic test of economic justice is what happens to the most vulnerable groups in society." The Latin American Council of Churches (CLAI) has observed that "paying off debts, which in many cases are unjust, with the sacrifice of the people is submitting them to a slow death". Referring to the "preferential option for the poor", the US Catholic bishops spoke in their well-known 1986 pastoral letter "Economic Justice for All" of the scandal that it is "the poorest people who suffer most from the austerity measures required when a country seeks the IMF 'seal of approval'".

Many church statements and reports observe that those who suffer from foreign debt are not the people who contracted the loans or benefited from them. Governments of debtor countries bear a share of the responsibility, but many factors are beyond their control: "Debtor countries had no say in the subsequent variation of the value of the dollar or in fixing high real interest rates... Why should the poor pay the consequences of such an unjust international economic order?", asked the WCC Central Committee.

The Methodist bishops of Latin America also pointed out in a 1985 statement that "foreign debt is the result of unjust economic relationships, a situation of domination and dependence, and at the same time an instrument of oppression... The massive debts of Latin America... are the pretext for maintaining debtor countries under economic and thus political control." Hence, according to a 1989 report of the Evangelical Lutheran Church in Tanzania (ELCT), "the challenge of the debt crisis lies in redefining the issue from one which is described in purely financial terms to one where basic social justice is seen to be at stake".

Some statements distinguish between legitimate and illegitimate debt. The Methodist bishops of Latin America contend that

> just as it is morally imperative to repay all legitimate debts, it is also ethically legitimate and a proper exercise of national sovereignty for nations affected to revise, condemn and even refuse to pay, in whole or in part, any illegitimate debts, or debts on which such extortionate rates of interest are charged as to endanger the lives of their citizens and the stability of democratic governments (Exod. 22:25, Ezek. 22:12).

A 1986 message from the YMCA in Argentina echoed this: "We have doubts about the legitimacy of the total debt, whose origins are not clear enough, and which was also undertaken by an illegitimate government."

As a matter of justice, the rich should share in the cost of adjustment, says the WCC Central Committee. In its 1987 document "At the Service of the Human Community", the Pontifical Commission Justice and Peace adds:

> In order to emerge from the international debt crisis, the various partners must agree on an equitable sharing of the adjustment efforts and the necessary sacrifices, taking into account the priority to be given to the needs of the most deprived peoples. It is the responsibility of the countries that are better off to assume a larger share.

There have been many statements by churches and ecumenical bodies calling for a total or partial cancellation of foreign debt. Brazilians and Tanzanians, for example, asked in 1989 that their foreign debts be cancelled. The Church of Norway bishops had adopted a similar position already in 1979. Like the WCC Central Committee, the US Roman Catholic bishops also suggested an outright cancellation of foreign debts of poor countries. The African Synod of Roman Catholic Bishops in April 1994 made a strong appeal to their counterparts in the North to challenge governments to cancel debts, improve conditions of trade and provide more effective aid.[15] The Methodist Bishops of Latin America have gone even further, asking for reparations for the centuries-long plunder of natural resources and exploitation of human labour. Most church documents, however, distinguish between the poorest countries and those who are a bit better off. The final document of the first European Ecumenical Assembly (Basel 1989), for example, called for a "lightening of the debt burden of the poor countries", but most statements follow the line of the synod of the United Church of Christ in the USA, which asked in a 1989 statement for a "major debt elimination for the poorest countries".

Appeals for substantial reform of the Bretton Woods institutions have come from the Roman Catholic bishops in the USA and church leaders in the Philippines.[16] The IMF must be "restructured to include greater participation on the part of poorer nations", says the United Church of Christ in the USA; and a Canadian ecumenical coalition adds that human rights and basic needs must be included in IMF conditionality. The WCC Central Committee identified four principles for restructuring the international financial system: universality (no discrimination against countries which do not follow neo-liberal economic policies), equitable representation (voting power should more closely reflect the distribution of population among countries), accountability and a fair reward for labour.

Most church documents recognize that the monetary system must be seen in the broader international economic context. The Pontifical Commission Justice and Peace speaks about the need to modify those rules of international trade which hinder a more just distribution of the fruits of growth. The Philippine bishops dispute the idea that international trade is naturally beneficial for poor countries, noting that "an open market is biased towards those with greater purchasing power... and with greater capital (such as the transnational corporations)". And the Evangelical Church in Germany states that it will be impossible to solve the debt problem without overcoming the increasing protectionism of industrial countries, especially in product areas where developing countries are competitive.[17]

Statements and reports like these have served as the basis for involvement by churches and church-related organizations in numerous actions.[18] Not all of these actions have come from circles one would readily consider "activist". For example, after a meeting of the WCC Plenary Commission on Faith and Order in Tanzania in August 1996, a group of church leaders from the UK wrote to the British Minister for Overseas Development, pleading for government action to help Tanzania in view of its $7 billion debt burden. Also in 1996, a group of Christians in the United Kingdom launched the Jubilee 2000 Campaign to remit the "unpayable backlog of debt" of the poorest countries by the year 2000. Although the campaign began as an initiative of Christians, it receives broad international support from people of different persuasions.

Providing effective debt relief to the 20 worst affected countries would cost less than building one Stealth bomber and roughly equivalent to building the Euro-Disney theme park in France. The relatively meagre financial costs contrast sharply with the appalling human costs of inaction.[19]

NOTES

1 Cheryl Payer, *The Debt Trap: The IMF and the Third World*, New York, Monthly Review Press, 1974, p.219.
2 *Third World Economics*, Feb. 1996.
3 Cf. the UN's *Human Development Report 1997*, p.9.
4 *The Economist*, 28 Oct. 1995.
5 Susan George and Fabrizio Sabelli, *Faith and Credit: The World Bank's Secular Empire*, Harmondsworth, UK, Penguin, 1994, p.5; John Mihevic, *The Market Tells Them So: The World Bank and Economic Fundamentalism in Africa*, London, Zed Books, 1995.
6 Advisory Group on Economic Matters, *The International Financial System: An Ecumenical Critique*, Geneva, WCC, 1985, p.56.
7 Alfred Gugler, "Creative Debt Relief: The Swiss Debt Reduction Facility", in John Cavanagh, Daphne Wysham and Marcos Arruda, eds, *Beyond Bretton Woods: Alternatives to the Global Economic Order*, London, Pluto Press, 1994, describes the campaign launched by NGOs in Switzerland in 1991 to mark the country's 700th anniversary by setting up a SFr. 700 million debt relief fund to write off commercial and bilateral debt in low-income countries.
8 Daniel D. Bardlow and Claudio Grossman, "Adjusting the Bretton Woods Institutions to Contemporary Realities", in Jo Marie Griesgraber and Bernhard G. Gunter, eds, *Development: New Paradigms and Principles for the 21st Century*, London, Pluto Press, 1996.
9 Bob Goudzwaard, *Poor in the World Economy* (CCPD occasional study pamphlet no. 3), Geneva, WCC, 1989.
10 For a discussion of the Tobin Tax see Mahbub ul Haq, Inge Kaul and Isabelle Grunberg, eds, *The Tobin Tax: Coping with Financial Volatility*, Oxford, Oxford U.P., 1996.
11 Cf. Lisa Jordan, "The Bretton Woods Challenges", in Griesgraber and Gunter, *op. cit.*
12 Reginald Green, "Reflections on Attainable Trajectories", in *ibid.*, p.40.
13 Cf. Roy Culpeper, "Multilateral Development Banks", in *ibid.*
14 For an argument that all interest is contrary to God's will see Michael Schluter, *The Old Testament Ban on Interest: Its Relevance for Reform of Britain's Industrial Structure in the 1980s*, Cambridge, Jubilee Centre, n.d.

74

[15] Cf. Pete Henriot, "What For? The Structural Adjustment Programme in Africa", *SEDOS Bulletin*, Vol. 27, no.10, 1995.

[16] "Response to the Pastoral Letter of the Roman Catholic Bishops in the USA by the Ecumenical Bishops Forum of the Philippines", *NCCP Newsletter*, 1985.

[17] *Bewältigung der Schuldenkrise: Prüfstein der Nord-Süd Beziehungen*, a position paper of the church development service of the Evangelical Church in Germany, no. 23, Hanover, EKD, 1988.

[18] For analyses of church statements on economic issues see the references in the Introduction, note 1 above.

[19] Cf. the UNDP *Human Development Report 1997*, p.93.

6. Work, Employment and Unemployment

The most violated article of the Universal Declaration of Human Rights may be Article 23: "everyone has the right to work, to free choice of employment, to just and favourable conditions of work, and to protection against unemployment."

In the rich OECD countries, unemployment affects 35 million people, and there are another 4 million or so who do not register as unemployed because they have given up hope of finding an acceptable job. Millions of others are employed only part-time. In Central and Eastern Europe, unemployment has ballooned (from zero) since the start of reforms in 1990, and wage employment has been falling sharply. Many Southern countries are struggling to expand employment fast enough to keep up with their growing populations, especially in urban areas.

Since there is no universally accepted definition of unemployment, national statistics cannot simply be added together to arrive at a precise figure for unemployment worldwide. Official unemployment statistics in most Southern countries do not adequately cover unemployment in rural areas or in the urban informal sector (for example, street vendors). In Northern countries, the growing clandestine employment also escapes the statistician.

Unemployment is spread unevenly. Youth unemployment is 20 percent in France and 25 percent in Ireland and Italy. Almost half of Spaniards under 24 are out of work. The unemployment rate among indigenous people in Canada is about 20 percent – twice that for other Canadians; in the United States, the rate for African Americans is twice that for whites. Unemployment figures for men and women in the United Kingdom are 9.5 percent for white men and 6.5 percent for white women; the corresponding figures for men and women from ethnic minorities are 20 percent and 17 percent. For Bangladeshi men and women, the unemployment rate is 40 percent.[1]

In the South, unemployment or underemployment means absolute poverty, hunger, illiteracy, poor health and a short life expectancy. In the North, it is often accompanied by social exclusion, alcoholism and drug abuse, crime, depression, disintegrating families and communities, sometimes even suicide. What was said by the ecumenical conference on Church, Community and State in Oxford in 1937 remains true today: unemployment

> tends to create in the mind of the unemployed person a sense of uselessness, or even of being a nuisance, and to empty his life of any meaning... This situation cannot be met by measures of unemployment assistance, because it is the lack of significant activity which tends to destroy human self-respect.

Conventional recipes

Unemployment emerges when the number of people looking for paid jobs exceeds the jobs available. This imbalance can be interpreted in two ways: either the number of paid jobs and the demand for workers is too low, or the number of people looking for those jobs is too high. Conventional wisdom has it that the number of paid jobs will increase when there is economic growth, when the labour market is made more flexible, and when wages are reduced, since cheaper labour automatically leads to more jobs.

Policies over the last 50 years have focused on accelerating economic growth. This has resulted in a fivefold increase in global GNP since 1950. Yet global unemployment is at its highest level since the great depression of the 1930s. While rapid economic growth has been accompanied by increased employment opportunities in some countries, much of this growth has generated little employment. Pakistan's real GDP grew by about 6.3 percent a year from 1975 to 1992, but employment increased by only 2.4 percent. India and Egypt had similar experiences. In Ghana between 1986 and 1991, GDP grew by 4.8 percent while employment *dropped* by more than 13 percent. In the European Union, unemployment has been rising since 1974, reaching about 11 percent in 1996, despite continued economic growth. Obviously, economic growth in itself is not an adequate medicine against unemployment.

The issue of flexible wages and a flexible labour market is more complicated. Employers may indeed be discouraged to hire people when wages are high and it is difficult to dismiss them. Hence, some argue for more flexible labour laws and a low minimum wage or none at all. Statistically, this approach seems to be successful in the United States, where the unemployment rate, fluctuating around 6 percent, is significantly lower than in most countries in the European Union, which have stuck to relatively high minimum wages and stricter labour laws.

But there is another side to this. Flexible wages and labour markets lead to higher wage inequalities; a cut in the minimum wage for young workers will reduce wages at the bottom while leaving top pay untouched. Three out of five US workers saw their real wages fall during the 1980s. Family incomes continued to grow because people worked longer hours and more women worked. Under flexible conditions, more work is likely to be temporary and precarious as it is easier to lose a job quite suddenly. Many of the jobs created are low-quality positions in the service sector, without security and without a future. Flexibility may lead to more people having a job and being included in one way or another in economic life. But it also leads to greater polarization and less social cohesion as income gaps widen. The good news about flexible labour markets is that they may create more jobs; the bad news is that you need two or three of those jobs to support a family.

Women and work

Much of the work done in society is unpaid and unrecorded – and thus unrecognized and unvalued. This is especially true of work in the household and in the community, most of which is done by women. In Northern countries, roughly two-thirds of women's total work time – compared to a third of men's – is unrecorded. In the South the proportion is similar for women, but for men it declines to less than a quarter. Thus men receive the lion's share of income and their economic contribution is recognized, while most of the work of women is not compensated or acknowledged. The UN Development Programme estimates that, in addition to the US$23 trillion in recorded world output in 1993, household and community work accounted for another US$16 trillion – of which women contributed $11 trillion.

In most countries women do more work than men. According to the UN's *Human Development Report 1996*, women's work burden in Japan is about 7 percent higher than men's, in Austria 11 percent higher, in Italy 28 percent higher. In the South women's share of the workload averages about 13 percent higher than men's share, and in rural areas 20 percent higher. In rural Kenya, for example, women do 35 percent more work than men. Indian women work 69 hours a week, while men work 59. Nepalese women work 77 hours, men 56. If women's unpaid work were properly valued, they would in most societies probably emerge as the major contributors to livelihood. A WCC report states that the reality of women's work lives requires rewriting the prevailing definitions of work to redress the sex bias in statistics and data-gathering.[2]

While many Northern countries have made progress in reducing the gap between women's and men's earnings, discrepancies remain. Women often earn much less than men because they hold low-paying jobs or work in the informal sector or are paid less than men for equal work. According to the UN Development Programme, the average female wage in many countries is only three-fourths of the male wage in the non-agricultural sector. Women are often treated as a permanent pool of cheap reserve labour that can be shifted back and forth between the home and the labour market as required. Special employment problems are encountered by minority women who face the dual oppression of racism and sexism.

In the formerly centrally planned economies of Central and Eastern Europe, women often had a strong position in the labour market, though many had to carry a double burden as homemakers and workers. Since 1990, however, many well-educated women have lost their jobs and suffer disproportionately from the economic malaise in most of those countries.

Technological developments

A common explanation for the phenomenon of jobless growth is the development of labour-saving technologies. But while millions of jobs have evidently been destroyed by machines since the industrial revolution, millions of other jobs have been created. In the long run, history suggests, new technologies have a small impact on the overall level of employment but a large impact on the relative demand for different types of workers.

New technologies in the past have mainly displaced manual workers, reducing or eliminating drudgery and thus having a liberating and humanizing influence on society, as well as bringing increased prosperity for millions of people. Jobs lost in one economic sector were eventually compensated by employment created in other sectors.

However, the persons losing their jobs cannot always find employment in the newly emerging economic sectors. It is not easy for a dismissed steelworker to become a computer specialist. Recent technological developments have increased the demand for highly skilled jobs and reduced the need for low-skilled labour while the wage gap between high- and low-skilled workers has widened. It is estimated that by the year 2020, less than 2 percent of the entire global workforce will still be engaged in factory work, leading to the virtual elimination of the blue-collar, mass assembly line worker from the production process.[3] This shift from mass to elite labour forces may be the root of the phenomenon of jobless growth, distinguishing work in the emerging Information Age, both qualitatively and quantitatively, from that in the outgoing Industrial Age.

Jeremy Rifkin predicts:

> We are rapidly approaching a historic crossroads in human history. Global corporations are now capable of producing an unprecedented volume of goods and services with an ever-smaller workforce. The new technologies are bringing us into an era of near worker-less production at the very moment in world history when population is surging to unprecedented levels. The clash between rising population pressures and falling

job opportunities will shape the geopolitics of the emerging high-tech global economy well into the next century.[4]

Between 1995 and 2010, Rifkin says, the South will add more than 700 million women and men to its workforce – more people than made up the entire labour force of the North in 1990. The need for jobs in the South dwarfs the number of jobs that are being created. Worldwide, more than a billion jobs will have to be created over the next ten years to provide an income for all the new job entrants. With robotics and automation eliminating jobs in every industry and sector, the likelihood of creating enough work for the hundreds of millions of new entrants into the job market appears slim.

The South has long attracted activities that are labour-intensive, taking advantage of the low wages in their countries. But as labour-saving technologies continue to shrink the percentage of the total production bill which goes to wages, the cost advantage of cheap Southern labour becomes less and less important. While cheap labour may still provide a competitive edge in industries such as textiles and electronics, machines are rapidly replacing cheap manual labour in other economic sectors.

At the same time, the position of the South as a producer of raw materials is being undermined by technology as more and more raw materials are replaced by other products. Artificial sweeteners have seriously reduced the income of sugar cane producers; satellites eliminate the need for tonnes of copper wire; oil-based products substitute for rubber – to mention just a few examples.

Chemical companies are investing heavily in indoor tissue-culture production, hoping to replace traditional agricultural production – another stronghold of Southern export products, especially in Africa. For example, vanilla can be produced from plant-cell cultures in laboratories at a fraction of the cost of natural vanilla. This will seriously affect the small island countries of Madagascar, Reunion and the Comores, where over 98 percent of the world's vanilla beans are grown. Proponents argue that this new technology reduces land use, soil erosion, use of agrochemicals and energy and transportation costs. Production can be regulated to daily market demand and is not subject to the uncertainties of climate, plant diseases, workers' demands and political instability. But the impact on farmers, especially in the South, could be catastrophic.

Global competition

Many observers see intensified global competition as the second major culprit in the decline in the number of jobs. To be competitive, companies shed jobs through automation, "leaner production" and exporting jobs to places where labour costs are lower. Workers are squeezed between automation on the one hand and a global competitive labour pool on the other. Not surprisingly, the influence of trade unions in most countries is weakening.

There are indeed indications that jobs of unskilled workers in the Northern countries may migrate to lower-wage countries. German companies, for example, expect to employ at least 300,000 more people abroad in the coming years – mainly in the lower-wage countries of Central and Eastern Europe. And a French report estimates that France, where unemployment is already high, could lose 2.5 million jobs to lower wage countries.[5]

But the consequences of this are less clear-cut than the figures suggest. For example, the increase of imports by the rich OECD countries from Asia is more or less compensated by their exports to Asia. Overall, the effects may balance each other out; certain economic sectors will gain while others will lose. An active government policy is necessary to correct the cleavages which result from these dynamics. In general, the argument that technological developments are the main reason for jobless growth is more convincing than the argument that increased international trade is the main culprit.

The object of government policy can hardly be to prevent technological developments. The real issue is how to manage changes so as to enhance justice. Not every type of work can or should be preserved, especially if the quality of the job is poor and it provides low levels of fulfilment and self-realization. Nevertheless, it is also the task of governments, in cooperation with business and civil society, to assure that those who lose their jobs will not lose their livelihoods as well.

Leisure or un(der)employment?

In Europe, the percentage of an average person's total life spent on paid work declined from 56 percent a century ago to 18 percent today. As the ratio between free time and working time is reversed, the question arises whether working time will become marginal and free time will replace material accumulation as the critical value and overriding goal of society. Will this free time take the form of unemployment or of leisure?

In a number of Northern countries this phenomenon is accompanied by two contradictory trends. On the one hand, while working hours are reduced, much useful and needed work remains undone, for example in the care sector of society. On the other hand, while many people are working less or are underemployed or unemployed, others are "overemployed" in the sense of working excessive overtime and being under high stress. This is of course true for many people in Southern countries who must work excessively in order to survive. But also in the United States, with its relatively flexible labour market, people are working more rather than less. The amount of leisure enjoyed by the average US citizen has shrunk by 37 percent since 1973. The average workweek, including commuting time, has increased from less than 41 hours to nearly 47. Some work harder of their own free will; others are forced to work more because real wages have fallen – they work harder for less pay.

While the picture is complicated and contradictory, in all situations technological developments result in a situation in which the same amount of goods or services can be produced with less labour. While labour-saving technologies should free people for greater leisure, they too often lead to growing under- and unemployment and further polarization.

Sharing work

If the choice is between more unemployment and more leisure, the productivity gains resulting from introducing labour-saving technologies will have to be shared in order to establish an equitable distribution of the fruits of technological progress. Rather than reducing the work force, Northern countries should shorten the workweek. Fears that this will be too costly and endanger the ability to compete are contradicted by some recent experiments.

In 1993 Volkswagen, Europe's largest automobile producer, adopted a four-day workweek to save 31,000 jobs that might otherwise have been lost as a result of a combination of increased global competition and new labour-saving technologies. This decision, which was supported by the workers, made Volkswagen the first transnational corporation to move to a 30-hour workweek. Although wages were reduced by 20 percent, the workers accepted this policy as an equitable alternative to mass permanent layoffs.

In Grenoble, France, Hewlett-Packard adopted a four-day workweek while at the same time deciding to keep the plant running seven days a week instead of five days. Workers now have to work in shifts, but on the average they work nearly six fewer hours a week than before, while keeping the same wage. As a result, production has tripled.[6]

In the Danish city of Aarhus, three municipal employees shared their work with one unemployed person while getting one week free a month. Sharing the sum total of three salaries and the unemployment benefits thus saved, and taking lower income tax into account, their net wages are 95 percent of the previous level. The employees get 12 weeks free and one unemployed person is provided with a job.[7]

Workfare

After a period in which it became a well-established custom – at least in Northern countries – to provide welfare to the jobless and others without an adequate income, we seem to be entering a period in which benefits for the jobless will be linked to the obligation to perform some kind of work. In such arrangements, called workfare, the state requires those receiving welfare payments to do work in the public sector such as basic health care or cleaning up public spaces.

Opposition to workfare comes from both ends of the political spectrum. Those on the right have resisted the idea of the state as "employer of last resort", arguing that it would mean the "nationalization of jobs". Those on the left fear that compulsion will create resentment and raise questions about how the state will be able to find the new jobs necessary to put to work all those who are presently unemployed. Public sector unions worry that workfare will undermine their position, as it is unlikely that those on workfare will join these unions and few "normal" jobs in the public sector will be available. Others ask how people will find satisfaction in jobs that do not offer merit pay and promotion opportunities; and some even refer to workfare as "slave labour".

Despite the objections, the idea of workfare seems to be catching on, since many people believe that welfare destroys the incentive for unemployed persons to look actively for a job. According to this line of reasoning – contested by many – the welfare benefits system adds to unemployment even if it eases the suffering of its victims. Workfare overcomes this disincentive by making benefit recipients work, bringing them back into the marketplace, which makes both economic and moral sense. Being on workfare reduces the chances for exclusion and gives people the feeling that they are useful members of society, thereby restoring their motivation, self-esteem and self-confidence.

The idea of workfare is furthest developed in the United States, where the responsibility for administering welfare benefits lies with the states rather than the federal government. Block grants are made to the states, which are required to oblige many welfare recipients to do some kind of work. Most recipients will be cut off after two years, and there is a lifetime limit of five years. This scheme has resulted in a 24 percent drop in the number of welfare recipients. In some states the reduction was very high: 54 percent in Wisconsin and 68 percent in Wyoming. The significance of these figures may be exaggerated by the overall drop in unemployment rates and the fact that it is the more easily employable persons on the welfare rolls who have responded to the workfare pressure. Such a rate of success is not likely to be sustained as the welfare list is more and more populated by the illiterate, drug addicts and the mentally disturbed.

Experience has shown that only a small proportion of those who go through workfare programmes are actually able to find a job in the private sector. This seems to contradict the idea of workfare as a kind of trampoline bouncing unemployed people back into social inclusion through "re-employment". While more emphasis on providing relevant re-training and re-education may contribute towards finding a solution, the short-run costs of this will be higher. The challenge is to develop policies which favour poor people but avoid permanent dependency on the state.

The trend towards privatization has also affected the administration of welfare and workfare programmes. In the US state of Texas, plans are being implemented which will eventually place almost every aspect of welfare – from determining eligibility to making payments to preventing fraud – in private hands. Texans who claim state-financed income support, health care, food coupons, job-training, drug-rehabilitation or pregnancy-prevention may never see a civil servant. Many social programmes which used to be the prerogative of government or charity will be in private hands.

Work and environment

The classic opposition between labour and capital has dominated most political-economic discussions of work over the years. Recently another tension has taken on growing importance: that between labour and production on the one hand and the natural environment on the other. In short, promoting economic growth and increasing production to combat unemployment can put an extra strain on the natural environment. How is the choice to be made between more jobs and environmental sustainability? Are we condemned to consume more in order to guarantee the level of economic growth necessary to create enough employment? Can "green unemployment" – caused by closing environmentally unsound factories – be compensated by creating "green employment" which safeguards the natural environment?

One suggestion for improving the quality of the environment and at the same time increasing the level of employment is to change radically the relative prices of labour and consumption. This can be done by lowering the taxes on labour – of which we want more – and increasing taxes on goods and services which are harmful for the environment ("eco-taxes"). Studies have indicated that such "win-win" situations do exist, although the advantages are not very large. Employment effects are positive but less than one percent. The effects on the gross domestic product range from a decrease of 0.7 percent to an increase of 0.5 percent.[8] In a globalizing economy, the positive effects of such a measure can be enhanced if more countries decide to change their fiscal regimes.

Concepts of work

Understandings of work are often related to religious convictions. Infuential within the Christian tradition have been the curse pronounced at the Fall that human beings shall work "by the sweat of their face" (Gen. 3:17-20), the concept of work as divine service, as in the monastic tradition, the idea of work as a vocation and a duty, as in much of the Protestant "work ethic", and the notion that through work human beings are co-creators with God.

Although biblical times were much different from our own, the Bible gives a few pointers relevant to today's situation. The concept of work as participation in God's creation is based on Genesis 2:15, which tells how the human being was placed in the Garden of Eden "to till it and keep it". Work is thus seen as creative activity. Its oppressive side is introduced as the consequence of the Fall (Gen. 3). But Genesis 1:26-28 has long served as the central text for a Christian understanding of work in general and the relation between work and nature in particular. The text states that human beings are created in the image of God and that the purpose of their work is to "subdue" the earth and to "have dominion" over other living creatures. Having dominion has often been misinterpreted as domination, with disastrous effects on the natural environment. And the story of the Tower of Babel (Gen. 11:1-10) illustrates how work and technology can be perverted into a means for human self-aggrandizement and self-glorification. Division rather than unity was the result.

Deuteronomy 26:6-8, in combination with Exodus 1:13-14, has been interpreted as biblical criticism of forced labour and slavery. The prophets denounce those who do not pay fair wages (cf. Jer. 22:13). Well known, and also relevant for today is the commandment to work for six days but to rest on and keep holy the seventh day, the Sabbath; work cannot be continuous (Ex. 20:8) and there should be a rhythmic alternation between work and worship.

A beautiful vision of work is given in the book of Isaiah:

> They shall build houses and inhabit them;
> they shall plant vineyards and eat their fruit.
> They shall not build and another inhabit;
> they shall not plant and another eat...
> My chosen shall long enjoy the work of their hands.
> They shall not labour in vain... (Isa. 65:21-24).

The concept of work as such is not central in the New Testament. The parable of the workers in the vineyard could be interpreted as a call to provide work to those who are willing and able to work (Matt. 20:1-16). Paul emphasizes that no one should live at the expense of others (Acts 20:34; 2 Thess. 3:7-9), and that through work the weak should be supported (Acts 20:35).

During the time of the church fathers, the Greeks and the Romans considered labour-related activities – artisanal or agricultural – degrading. A free human being was supposed to engage in ethical, philosophical and political activities. True citizens ought not to work. The church fathers went against this tide, emphasizing like Paul that idleness is wrong, as it is linked with exploitation of others.

In the 16th century, Martin Luther identified with farmers, fisherfolk and craftsmen and criticized monks and church hierarchs who, following Aristotle and Thomas Aquinas, valued the contemplative life over work. While Luther saw labour as a duty and a vocation, John Calvin emphasized that it is a means to serve God. Both Reformers warned against accumulating riches by focusing one's entire life on work. At the same time, they condemned laziness.

Roman Catholic social teaching in the 20th century has emphasized the dignity of workers and thereby also the dignity of work. Work is part of everybody's vocation, according to Pope Leo XIII in *Rerum Novarum* (1891). Pope John Paul II has picked up the idea that human beings are co-creators with God. His encyclical *Laborem Exercens* (1981) gives work an eschatological meaning: through work human beings contribute to the liberation of humanity.

We saw earlier that ecumenical discussion of work began with a focus on unemployment. Already in 1924, the Conference on Christian Politics, Economics and Citizenship, whose driving force was William Temple, later Archbishop of Canterbury, called unemployment morally unacceptable. COPEC was organized in preparation for the Universal Christian Conference on Life and Work (Stockholm 1925), which spoke of the "tremendous question of unemployment" and sent its message to the workers of the world "in the name of the Son of Man, the Carpenter of Nazareth". The great depression influenced the world conference on Church, Community and State (Oxford 1937), whose message speaks of unemployment as sapping people's strength of body, mind and spirit. The WCC's second assembly (Evanston 1954) spoke of society's obligation to provide all its members an opportunity to work.[9] Echoing this statement, a more recent WCC report says: "Every person has to have the opportunity to be a co-worker with God. Therefore the Christian commitment is to full and fully adequate employment, here and now and not in the New Jerusalem or in the year 2000."[10]

Looking back over the 20th century ecumenical debate about work, theologian Lukas Vischer concludes that "aside from a few incomplete overtures, there was no suggestion that the phenomenon of unemployment invites a rethinking of work itself".[11] Yet, such a reassessment is urgent. What might be some of its elements?

Work for life

We have already suggested that the equation of work with employment, specifically with recorded wage employment, is inadequate. For example, family members may work in a family enterprise without receiving a wage. But the issue is more fundamental: defining work as "having a paid job" creates the impression that unpaid activities do not constitute a useful contribution to society and ignores the fact that "productive labour" could not exist without unpaid "non-productive" labour such as volunteer community work and rearing children.

As we have seen, much of this work is done by women, and conventional views on work and employment thus disregard the essential role played by women in society. So it is important to extend the concept of work beyond recorded wage employment to include all ways of securing a livelihood. A job is an activity performed in exchange for payment; a livelihood is a means of "making a living" – or of supporting life.

If promoting life becomes the centrepiece of our economic thinking, our views on work, labour and employment will change drastically. In such a vision, the real need is not necessarily for more paid jobs. Rather, the focus is on promoting work for justice, peace and the safeguarding of God's creation, thereby enhancing life. Contrary to paid jobs, such work is not scarce; everywhere there is a need to strengthen the bonds of families and communities in civil society and to protect the natural environment. Work to make a living, to promote life, is the foundation of just, participatory and sustainable societies which avoid both too much external dependence and local isolation.

Some will object that such a vision of work for life is remote indeed from the reality in which the vast majority of humankind finds itself today. For most people, having gainful employment is an absolute necessity and indeed the only way to secure livelihood. Losing such employment means deprivation and misery and is, in the end, a threat to life itself. For one struggling to survive, let alone lead a decent, dignified and human life, romantic visions of work are useless, even insulting.

Nevertheless, global developments force us to think differently. Just as horses gave way to tractors in agricultural production (and are now mainly used for leisure), human beings may be more and more replaced by machines and computers as the most important means of production. In this light, a call for full employment – in the sense of a 40-hour workweek – becomes anachronistic. A WCC report states:

> We need to prepare for a social structure in which only part of the working population will be needed to produce all the goods and services (i.e. an extension to the industrial economy of a phenomenon which already exists in agriculture). We must do away with the single, salaried and full-time job syndrome and promote a pluralistic society based on plural activities for its members.[12]

The idea of remunerated work as the most important basis for participation and integration in society is increasingly questionable. The perception of citizenship changes if it is not only people with paid jobs who are seen as useful citizens. A more comprehensive concept of citizenship is needed, expressed in all domains of society, affirming human dignity, enhancing the quality of life and improving participation and inclusion in community life. This view sees the purpose of work as building sustainable and inclusive communities in which the different gifts of every member of society are contributed and recognized. In such communities – which could be called the social economy – people are increasingly likely to address personal and societal needs that can no longer be dealt with in the marketplace. Women and men can explore new roles and responsibilities, find a new meaning in their lives and shape new forms of solidarity and new concepts of citizenship.

In the social economy, voluntary organizations take up the task of providing more and more basic services as the state is retreating. Churches and many others are already engaged in projects to support the unemployed and in programmes for retraining and self-employment. In many countries, "soup kitchens" have been set up to provide food for the poor. In a number of Western European countries, Local Employment Trading Systems (LETS) are emerging. Members of LETS work for one another and are paid in accounting units or points instead of money, building up positive and negative balances ("I cut your hair, you repair my car"). Such arrangements create a barter economy operating in parallel with the conventional market economy and welfare system. More than 35,000 voluntary organizations in the South are involved in health care, literacy, advocacy, land reform and rural development. In Africa and Latin America many of these citizens' organizations have emerged from the churches. In the USA, the social economy already contributes more than 6 percent of the GNP (calculated in conventional terms) and is responsible for 10.5 percent of the total national employment.[13]

The social economy, built on a comprehensive concept of citizenship, is probably the most effective way to counter the forces of technological displacement, exclusion and fragmentation. Broadening loyalties and affiliations beyond the marketplace and the job may provide a much-needed antidote to the prevailing emphasis on unqualified growth, consumerism and materialism.

Although rapidly growing, the social economy is not likely to replace the global market economy in the foreseeable future, so that the two will probably exist side-by-side. To the extent that the system of paid jobs is the cornerstone of the social security system, other ways will have to be found to protect citizens from destitution, since the social economy is no guarantee against exclusion. Nevertheless, the emerging social economy is a sign of hope for those who are concerned about whether "the future will work". Creativity and political will are indispensable if this sign of hope is to be given a chance.

NOTES

[1] Cf. *Unemployment and the Future of Work: An Enquiry for the Churches*, London, Council of Churches for Britain and Ireland, 1997.

[2] R.H. Green, ed., *Labour, Employment and Unemployment: An Ecumenical Reappraisal*, Geneva, WCC, 1987, p.33.

[3] Jeremy Rifkin, "Re-envisioning Work: The Rebirth of the Civil Society", *Social Development*, Vol. 1, no.2, Dec. 1996.

[4] Jeremy Rifkin, *The End of Work: The Decline of the Global Labour Force and the Dawn of the Post-Market Era*, New York, Putnam, 1995, p.207.

[5] Annie Fouquet and Frederic Lemaitre, *Démystifier la Mondialisation de l'Economie*, Paris, Les Editions d'Organisation, 1997, p.79.

[6] Rifkin, *The End of Work*, p.225.

[7] Ilkka Sipilainen, "End of Work, Job-Sharing and Shortening of Working Time", in *The Future of Work in Europe*, report of a consultation of the Work and Economy Network of the European churches, Manchester, UK, Sept. 1996.

[8] Cf. Hans Opschoor, "Sustainable Growth and Employment", *The Ecumenical Review*, Vol. 48, no.3, July 1996, p.341.

[9] Cf. *The Evanston Report: The Second Assembly of the WCC, 1954*, New York, Harper, 1954, p.167.

[10] R.H. Green, *op. cit.*, p.3.

[11] Lukas Vischer, "The Work of Human Beings As Creatures of God", *The Ecumenical Review*, Vol. 48, no.3, Jul. 1996.

[12] Theodor Leuenberger, "Global Trends in Employment: Problems and Strategies", in Howard Davis and David Gosling, eds, *Will the Future Work? Values for Emerging Patterns of Work and Employment*, Geneva, WCC, 1985, p.5.

[13] Jeremy Rifkin, "Re-envisioning Work", *loc. cit.*

7. Land: the Third Production Factor

Compared with capital and labour, the third production factor, land, receives little attention in either the media or in mainstream economics – and when it does, it is usually in connection with environmental issues.

The paramount importance of land and the resources it provides is underscored by a traditional principle of elementary economics: efficiency requires maximizing the productivity of the scarcest production factor. Over the long run, labour is reproducible, given resources and food; capital is reproducible, given resources and labour. But resources are a different matter. Some – especially minerals and fossil fuels – are not reproducible on human time-scales; and even renewable resources can be depleted if they are exploited beyond their capacity to reproduce. In the long run, therefore, resources/land would seem to be the scarcest production factor.[1]

Some theological ideas

In the Hebrew Bible, land plays a pre-eminent role. The people of Israel confessed that "the land belongs to Yahweh" (Psalm 24:1; usually translated "the earth is the Lord's"). The land belongs to God who freed the slaves and led them to the promised land. God is a God of liberation, freedom and justice, and God's land has to be managed in that spirit.

There is also a polemical aspect to this confession: the land does *not* belong to Baal or the other gods worshipped by surrounding peoples. At the same time there is a warning against those who think they own the land, especially against those who live in the city – which in the Hebrew Scriptures symbolizes power, oppression and monopoly.

Land is an integral part of the covenant between Yahweh and the people of Israel. The most radical expression of this covenantal ethic of land is the jubilee provision (Lev. 25) for returning land to its rightful owners every 50 years. Land should not be monopolized. Walter Brueggemann has observed that the ram's horn (*yobel*), which was blown to announce the jubilee year, was also blown when the walls of Jericho fell (Joshua 6). The sound which announces the jubilee is the same as that which breaks the military power and monopoly of the city and paves the way for a covenantal life.[2]

Because the land belongs to God, its fruits should be shared. Part of its produce should be given to the poor, the widows, the orphans, the strangers. The story of Ruth illustrates that living and working on the land not only brought rights but also entailed duties. In the Christian tradition, the eucharist exemplifies this sharing. Fruits of the land – wine and bread – are offered in thanksgiving to God, after which they are shared. But land, given by God to meet human needs, can also become an arena for human greed. Greed for land brings judgment (Isa. 5:8-9; 1 Kings 21). Land speculation and the coveting of land lead to injustice (Micah 2:1-5). Ruthless exploitation of small tenants by landlords is condemned (Amos 5:11).

These themes were also picked up by some of the church fathers. St Ambrose said: "You are not making a gift of what is yours to the poor persons, but you are giving them back what is theirs. You have been appropriating things that are meant to be for the common use of everyone. The earth belongs to everyone, not to the rich." St John Chrysostom was even more explicit: "God never made some rich and some poor. God gave the same earth for all. The whole earth is the Lord's and the fruits of the earth should be common to all."[3]

The understanding of land in the Hebrew Scriptures is thus central to the preservation of communities. When God's laws for the land are violated, communities disintegrate and injustice is done. The provision that the land should rest during the sabbath year indicates that it should not be exploited beyond its capacity to regenerate – if only because the preservation of human life depends on the land and on the resources it generates. Land, including soil, air and water, are given by God for the sustenance of all life. The close link between land and humanity, between soil and soul, is reflected in the fact that the Hebrew words for arable land (*adamah*) and humankind (*adam*) have the same root: the word *dam* (life-blood).[4]

Some indigenous theologians would go as far as to reformulate Psalm 24:1, "The earth is the Lord's", into "The earth is God". Many Christians would have difficulties with this interpretation, maintaining that while land and creation must be respected only God the Creator is worthy of worship.

In summary, land in the Hebrew Bible is the context of the covenant, and God continues to care for it (Deut. 11:12). A landless people – the Israelites – is invited to become landed and free (Deut. 6:20-23). The land is a safe place to dwell (Lev. 26:5-6), a place to grow food and mine resources needed for life (Deut. 8:7-10; Amos 9:13-15), a place to enjoy good things (Ex. 3:8; Eccles. 6:3). But while people are free to use, enjoy and benefit from the land, God retains ownership (Ps. 24:1; Lev. 25:23). Human beings serve as God's caretakers on the land. Land use is conditional on sharing, and we are to use it gratefully (Deut. 8:10) and sustainably (Deut. 22:6-7).

As Christianity developed, awareness of the link between God, people and land diminished – and when it has been emphasized, it has often brought exclusivistic and disastrous consequences, as in Nazi Germany and apartheid South Africa. More often, it seems, Christians have spiritualized the idea of the "promised land" as a reference to the coming reign of God, thus paving the way for a more instrumental view of land and nature. "Dominion" (Gen. 1:28) became domination, and salvation and redemption were applied only to human beings.

The farm crisis

The absence of a jubilee vision for the land is painfully felt by small farmers today. In the North as well as the South large-scale mechanized food production is forcing small producers out of business, resulting in rural unemployment and the degradation of the quality of rural life and communities. This in turn aggravates urbanization problems as jobless farmers and their families move to big cities in the hope of finding work. For example, within a lifetime, Brazil has shifted from a country whose population was 75 percent rural to one which is 75 percent urban. Between 1960 and 1980, some 2.5 million Brazilians migrated from the countryside to the cities as a result of the growing "modernization" of agriculture and the concentration of land ownership favouring large farms.

In the late 1960s and 1970s it was widely believed that technology and improved seed varieties, in combination with pesticides, herbicides and fertilizers, would solve many agricultural problems. In fact, the problems for which technological solutions were being sought were social and political problems of inequity. The Green Revolution benefited many farmers – especially the already wealthy ones – but where it was not accompanied by policies aimed at better access to land and other production factors for small farmers and landless rural workers the basic problem of inequity was not solved.

Of particular concern in the USA is the rapidly diminishing number of African American farmers – already an especially vulnerable group. On the whole, African American farmers depend more heavily on farming for an income than other farmers; yet they are losing their land to large farmers and agribusiness at a far greater rate. US churches have repeatedly asked the authorities to reverse the trend of loss of ownership of agricultural land by African Americans.

Small farmers commonly work 12-16 hours a day to scrape a living from a small plot of land. Often they have little or no reserves of food or money to carry them over lean seasons or years, let alone to purchase enough seeds, fertilizers and tools. Even when the harvest is good, inadequate storage facilities may mean that much of their produce is lost. To survive they may have to sell their animals or even their land, further limiting their capacity to grow food, or to borrow money from local lenders, often at exorbitant interest rates. Women are particularly affected. Although they constitute almost half of the agricultural labour force in Africa and Asia, and about one-third in Latin America and the Middle East, they are often ignored or even discriminated against in land and credit policies. In some societies, women do not even have the legal right to own land.

Forced by the immediate demands of survival, small farmers may exploit the land beyond its capacity to regenerate, resulting in soil exhaustion. Often the land on which they are forced to farm is already marginal, with thin and infertile soil, prone to erosion. Forests may be cut and burned for farmland, destroying delicate eco-systems.

Landless farmers

In his message to the World Food Council in 1984, WCC general secretary Philip Potter spoke of "the masses of landless rural labourers who work on other people's land, often under conditions of exploitation, humiliation and deprivation". In some parts of the world, landless farm workers make up a high percentage of the total workforce. Only during the height of the agricultural seasons can they find employment, and with the pitifully low wages they earn during this season they must provide for themselves and their families throughout the entire year.

The causes of landlessness are varied. Population pressure is an important factor, especially in many Asian countries. While population continues to grow, the supply of fertile land at best remains the same, and is often shrinking as cities expand and erosion due to the misuse of land, floods and other natural disasters sweeps away the topsoil. Traditional inheritance laws and customs may divide farms into ever-smaller plots. In many countries of the South, colonial land-holding patterns persist, excluding small farmers from vast areas of land – often of the best quality. In Latin America, for example, four-fifths of all cultivated land is taken up by large *latifundias*, while small farmers, who make up more than half of the rural population, have less than one-fifth. Land-tenure patterns favouring large firms may result from government policies geared to develop cash crops for export markets in order to earn foreign exchange. Yet another cause for landlessness is poverty itself, as land-owning small farmers are forced to sell their holdings to repay debts.

So far, landlessness has been a less serious problem in Africa than in other Southern continents. This is largely because of the customary tenure system on communal land, and because large tracts of potentially arable land are still available in many areas. But landlessness is growing in Africa as population increases; and the tragic events in Rwanda in 1994 also had their roots in this problem.

Brazil has the most inegalitarian structure of land owner-ship of any country in the world, with 0.8 percent of landowners holding 43 percent of the land and just 75 landowners (including TNCs) owning 7.3 percent. More than three-fifths of this land is unused except for speculation – traded like stocks and shares. While some 170 million hectares of viable agricultural land are held out of use by big landowners, 12 million Brazilian peasants are landless.

The *Sem Terra* movement of landless peasants is in the forefront of the struggle for a less unequal distribution of land in Brazil. Over the years, thousands of squatters have toppled fences to invade and occupy farms and ranches, often supported by Roman Catholic priests. In response landowners have organized their own militia to protect their land, and some of the land invasions have ended in blood-shed. During the past 10 years, 700 people have been mur-dered by private militia and even the police. Seldom if ever are investigations carried out. A WCC team visiting Brazil in 1996 described this as another example of impunity for crimes against the poor in Brazil and concluded that land reform is the vital ingredient in establishing meaningful democracy in Brazil.

Although most Brazilians live in towns, the *Sem Terra* movement has won huge political sympathy. Their march on the capital Brasilia in early 1997 turned into the biggest demonstration the government had ever faced. Under such pressure, the government pledged to grant land to 280,000 families in four years, increased taxes on unfarmed land and is speeding up expropriation procedures.

Similarly uneven land distribution is found in Guatemala, where the best cultivable land is found on the estates of agro-exporters, who also own most of the means of production for agriculture and stockbreeding. This minority produces and sells products which fetch the highest prices on the international markets – coffee, cotton, bananas and cattle – while the peasants, mostly indigenous people who own tiny plots of land, grow maize and beans under precarious circumstances. Thousands of Guatemalan peasants have died for trying to change these structures.

Land reform

There is no single global solution to the problems of small farmers and landless labourers, because their situations vary a great deal from one place to another. What is common to all contexts is that reducing poverty, improving access to land, water and other natural resources, credit and education, and equitable legislation are crucial factors in the search for solutions.

But despite its favourable consequences for food security and slowing the exodus from the countryside to the slums, land reform almost inevitably meets with fierce opposition from established power groups. Failure to implement land reform, however, can also lead to violent reactions. When Ecuador adopted a new land law in 1994 which virtually put an end to three decades of land reform, violent clashes broke out between indigenous communities and others protesting the opening of the market for land to big farmers and agro-industry. Similarly, farmers movements in India strongly opposed the undoing of land reform policies by various state governments in 1996 in order to allow TNCs and other big companies to buy agricultural land for growing export crops. The farmers also protested the privatization of water resources, the production of meat for export, and the monopolization of seeds as a result of the adoption of Trade Related Intellectual Property Rights (TRIPs) in the context of the World Trade Organization.

The situation in South Africa shows how awesome a task land reform can be. At least 3.5 million and perhaps as many as 7 million black South Africans were driven from their homes and land between 1913 and 1989. As white farms swelled in size, black lands became ever more crowded and overgrazed. By 1970 the average size of a white-owned farm in South Africa was 988 hectares (more than six times the size of the average farm in the US and Canada), while the average black farm was barely one hectare. The South African government's land reform scheme comes in three parts: (1) restoring to the original owners or their heirs any land confiscated since 1913; (2) redistributing to the black majority a total of 30 percent of the country's arable land; (3) modernizing tenure by giving tenant farmers who have lived on a white farm for more than a generation the right to buy themselves a decent patch.

The resistance by whites to this scheme is strong. Some declare that it amounts to "confiscation in reverse". Others warn that turning land over to small farmers will prompt a drop in farming output. Another problem is finding money to pay for the scheme and deciding who should foot the bill. Furthermore, much of the land being returned under the redistribution schemes is, like other land across Africa, held communally and administered by a chief. Banks are unwilling to treat communally held land as a collateral, which may prevent obtaining loans to improve agricultural production. The patriarchal inheritance system in some parts of South Africa means that if a man dies without sons, his land passes to his brother, not his wife. This can leave a widow without any land at all – in a country where women do most of the farm labour.

Similar obstacles have prevented the government of Zimbabwe from delivering on its promises for land redistribution. Where blacks have received their land back, they often do not have the knowledge and skills to till it. Land reform in favour of small farmers is further hampered by the current emphasis on capital-intensive agricultural production based on new seed varieties and more chemical fertilizers, pesticides and herbicides, requiring large capital investments which small farmers cannot afford.

Dams and land

A type of land loss which has become more prevalent in recent decades is that caused by the building of dams. The benefits of dams seem obvious at first glance. A dam creates electricity from water falling through its turbines, and the supply is replenished in perpetuity by nature without anything being used up or contaminated. The lake which forms behind a dam can allow a country to make the best use of water as a precious resource (for drinking, washing or irrigation) and can hold back water to prevent floods. The lake may be turned into a tourist attraction, stocked with fish and used as a fallback source of water in times of drought.

However, dams can also have serious disadvantages which are rarely if ever included in a dam's cost-benefit analysis. Even if they do not cause pollution, dams may cause considerable environmental damage; and they often force massive human resettlement. It is estimated that the building of large dams in various parts of the world has already driven some 4 million people off their ancestral lands. The massive Three Gorges dam which China began to build in 1994 will by itself displace up to 1.3 million people. These resettlements are almost always badly planned and executed. Often it is ethnic groups that have to leave their land. The new land they get in return is usually of lesser quality – leaving aside the attachment of indigenous people to their ancestral lands – and their new neighbours frequently see them as invaders into their land.

Consequently, protests against the building of dams have grown in recent years. Some large projects have been abandoned halfway through, and funding for new ones is becoming more and more difficult. Even the World Bank, once a major promoter of hydroelectric projects, has become more cautious.

The building of dams is often accompanied by brute force and bribery. Before the reservoir of the Chixoy Dam in Guatemala, funded by the World Bank, was filled in 1982, nearly 400 people resisting resettlement were massacred. The bank is now attempting to improve the living conditions of the survivors, who were never properly compensated for the economic losses caused by their resettlement. The Bank's own report on the Chixoy project said that "with hindsight it has proved to be an unwise and uneconomic disaster". The British government approved an aid package for the building of the Pergau dam in Malaysia in March 1988 on the understanding that the Malaysian military would buy Hawk fighter planes from Britain – this despite the fact that the British High Court declared such use of aid illegal and the National Audit Office warned that the hydroelectric scheme was not "prudent and economic".

Indigenous people and land

For indigenous peoples, land is of paramount importance. As a report to the WCC Central Committee in 1979 stated:

> The land is the essence of their being. It is their peoplehood, their nationhood. Through centuries of spiritual devotion to the creation, the indigenous people have developed social, cultural, religious and economic patterns of life which are in harmony with the rhythms of the land itself.

Because land is the living link between indigenous peoples and their ancestors, they are not only physically but also spiritually related to the land. Land is a unifying force, essential to all aspects of life – social, political, spiritual, cultural, economic. To separate indigenous peoples from their land is to deny their peoplehood. Places where ancestors are buried are sacred. Land cannot be a commodity that can be bought or sold; ultimately it belongs to the Creator. It cannot be compensated for with money or another piece of land. Communal rather than individual ownership characterizes indigenous land use.

Given such an understanding, Western colonialism and expansionism have spelled disaster for indigenous peoples all over the world. Ill-conceived notions of development, penetrating modernization and globalizing markets threaten their culture, their land and their very lives. The WCC Central Committee meeting in 1982 mentioned some examples:

> In Brazil, "Indian nations" are being forced from their lands and squeezed into isolated areas by new highway, mining and agricultural development projects. In Western Australia, a mining

boom is violating the cultural integrity and sacred sites of the Aboriginal people, while in northern parts of Canada, massive oil, gas and uranium projects threaten to destroy the fragile environment and the social fabric of the indigenous communities.

Besides the hunger for land to be used for farming, construction, mining and dams, the booming demand for timber is leading to further violations of the land rights of indigenous peoples. While prices of most agricultural commodities have been stable or have fallen, the price of tropical timber has rapidly risen, leading to further invasions of indigenous territories.

Indigenous people whose lands have been confiscated are even sometimes used as slaves. In 1992 there were reports that hundreds of forcibly relocated tribal people in Myanmar (formerly Burma) were being used as slave labour to build a railway in the country's northeast. The Kayah and Karen tribespeople, largely Christian migrant farmers, were relocated from the hills to the plains. Their homes and villages were then burned and their crops destroyed in an effort to prevent them from returning to their ancestral land.[5]

Indigenous land rights

The assumption that the Aboriginal peoples of Australia had no right to the land on which their ancestors had lived for 40,000 years before 1770, when Captain James Cook claimed the country on behalf of king George III, was enshrined in the doctrine of *terra nullius* (no man's land), which was long accepted by the courts. In effect this meant that they had no existence under British law; and not until 1967 did Australians decide in a referendum to recognize indigenous Australians as human beings to be counted in the census. In the Mabo case in 1992, the Australian High Court ruled that Aboriginal people had the right to claim native title to traditional lands, something never recognized before. In 1997, the High Court further decided that native title rights can co-exist with the rights of pastoralists. The fact that most of Australia's territory is now subject to native claims obviously worries farmers and mining companies.

Unlike Australia, Aotearoa New Zealand has always recognized, at least theoretically, that the indigenous Maori
(also known as the *tangata whenua* – "people of the land")
were there first. Their rights were enshrined in the Treaty of
Waitangi, negotiated in 1840 between the Maori representa-
tives of the North Island and the British Crown, which
guaranteed Maori rights to their economic, political, cultural
and spiritual *taonga* (treasures or possessions). Nevertheless,
since the Treaty was signed, these rights have been violated.
Only 3 million of the country's 66 million acres of land
remain in the hands of the Maori, who today represent 12
percent of the population. Since 1987, governments of
Aotearoa New Zealand have accepted the principle that
Maoris should be compensated for the violations of the
Treaty. Recognizing that land rights include water rights, the
government made an effort in 1992 to settle old disputes
about who owns the fishing grounds around the country by
supporting Maori participation in a joint-venture fishing
company.

The indigenous peoples of Brazil have one of the most
tragic histories of any of the world's indigenous peoples.
Since the first European invaders arrived some 500 years
ago, they have seen their lands stolen, their traditions
destroyed and their people murdered. In the Amazon region
more than 80 indigenous cultures have been wiped out since
the beginning of this century. Only recently has some hope
for their future appeared. In its new democratic constitution
of 1988 the Brazilian state finally agreed to recognize the
rights of indigenous peoples and to guarantee them permanent rights to the lands they traditionally occupied. Yet
although indigenous peoples living in "demarcated" areas
have the right to live according to their own customs and
laws, free from outside interference, their suffering continues
as loggers, ranchers, miners and other business interests continue to invade and illegally occupy indigenous lands.

The vast forests of Siberia are twice the size of the Amazon basin; and the growing pressure to exploit them is illustrated by the struggle of the Udege people against the logging

interests of the South Korean commercial giant Hyundai. In fact, many TNCs are trying to take advantage of the political chaos in post-communist Russia to negotiate contracts allowing them to exploit natural resources to the detriment of indigenous peoples in Russia.

Not that the Soviet period was favourable to these peoples. For example, the land of the Khanty people was widely polluted by clumsy large-scale Soviet oil extraction. The petroleum industry also brought an influx of people into their traditional areas: the population has grown from 100,000 to 1.5 million people since 1961; and the Khanty, who made up 25 percent of the population 25 years ago, are now only 1.8 percent. Until the 1930s, the Khanty were more or less autonomous. Under Stalin the state took over their reindeer herds, pasture land and hunting rights, forbade their nomadic way of life, murdered their shamans or threw them into concentration camps and sent their children to boarding schools. Today, pipelines carve through most of their territory, forests have been cut and burned, elk and reindeer have almost disappeared, oil leakages destroy the fish and water plants, and air pollution is causing a very high rate of illness. Increased sickness is also reported by the Nenets of the Arctic Sea, whose territory is close to the site of nuclear testing in the 1950s and 1960s.

Many North American Indian tribes are also waiting for justice. The Great Sioux Reservation covered 20 million acres in 1868. As precious raw materials have been found on their territory, the Sioux have been forced into an ever-smaller area and now occupy only 5.5 million acres. Most painful was the loss of the Black Hills, their most sacred ground, where they believe the first Sioux was put on earth. Unfortunately, gold was found there. In 1980, the US Supreme Court decided that the Sioux should be awarded US\$106 million as compensation for the land taken from them. Besides being an insult to the Sioux's religious convictions, the amount offered – less than \$1500 for each member of the Sioux nation – was a pittance compared to the billions of dollars' worth of coal, uranium, gold, copper, other precious metals and tourist income which have been and continue to be taken from the Black Hills.

These examples of the violation of the land rights of indigenous peoples could be multiplied many times over. Certain countries have however begun to recognize in law the right of indigenous populations to land ownership and to a system of land tenure different from that applying to the rest of the population. Indigenous peoples are organizing themselves at national, regional and international levels, and as a result the importance of establishing and preserving indigenous land rights is being increasingly stressed in resolutions and declarations adopted by international conferences, non-governmental organizations and church bodies. Most of these statements affirm the following basic principles:

- the special relationship of indigenous peoples to their land should be understood and recognized as basic to all their beliefs, customs, traditions and cultures;
- recognition should be given to the right of indigenous nations or peoples to the return of and control over sufficient and suitable land to enable them to live a dignified life in accordance with their own customs and traditions;
- ownership of land should include the control of all natural resources, and fully allow communal ownership of land, protected by law.

Mining

Churches have also taken up the cause of indigenous peoples through interventions, campaigns and solidarity actions. A recent example is support given by the WCC to a meeting in London in 1996 on the exploitation of indigenous peoples by mining companies. Among the chief concerns were the loss of land and the damage to health of indigenous people through mining. A Brazilian government decree of January 1996 was said to open up for "development" more than 300 indigenous areas, including some already reserved for indigenous peoples. The Timbishe Shoshone tribe in the US was reported to have been ordered by the federal government to give up for gold mining the last tiny pocket of their traditional homelands – 16.2 hectares in Death Valley, California. Advasi communities in India complained that iron, uranium, coal and bauxite mines were scarring their lands and polluting their rivers. Uranium mining and mercury (used in gold mining) are blamed for damaging women's health by harming the reproductive system.

The London meeting adopted a declaration seeking a fair deal from mining companies, including recognition of land rights, mining only with consent, protection of children's health, and an end to "violations of women's rights through the trafficking and trading of women" – a reference to organized prostitution in mining communities. The delegates also decided to form an alliance to plan a coordinated response to the increasing encroachment on their lands by mining companies.

One of the companies accused of violating the land rights of indigenous peoples was Australia's Broken Hill Proprietary (BHP), one of the world's largest mining conglomerates. For eight years, tribal villagers in Papua New Guinea had accused BHP of polluting their rivers with copper and gold mining waste from a mine situated high in the jungle-covered Star Mountains. Each year, 58 million metric tons of rock and powdery mining wastes flow down into the Ok Tedi River and then into the Fly River. The tribal villages hold that the waste has poisoned the Fly River and changed its course in some places, affecting the numbers and size of fish caught. Shortly after the London meeting, a BHP representative visited the WCC to announce an agreement between the tribal villagers and the company. BHP would pay some US$110 million to 30,000 landowners and may build an improved waste treatment facility and pipeline down from the mountains, a clean-up operation that would cost up to $360 million.

In 1996, BHP obtained Canadian government approval to construct a diamond mine, valued at $17 billion, some 300 km. northeast of Yellowknife in a fragile tundra area. Five lakes will be pumped dry to access the diamonds, and a sixth will be filled with billions of tonnes of mine tailings. The

Dene, Inuit and Innu people have raised serious concerns about the mine's potential impact on the eco-system, wildlife, and indigenous communities in the region.[7] It will be interesting to see whether the lessons BHP learned in Papua New Guinea will be applied to its mining operations in Canada.

Land, development and racism

About 25 years ago, the governor of Roirama in the Upper Amazon territory of Brazil moved the Yanomani people off their land into areas where they could hardly survive, declaring that "an area as rich as this – with gold, diamonds and uranium – is not able to afford the luxury of conserving a half a dozen Indian tribes who are holding back development."[8]

This statement reveals a fundamental idea, indeed belief, about what development and economics is about. Even if few people today would express this idea with such blatant insensitivity, the equation of "development" with economic growth and modernization persists. From this perspective, "underdevelopment" is primarily if not exclusively an economic problem. And since the problem is essentially economic, so is the solution. This does not mean that the theoreticians and practitioners of this type of development ignore non-economic factors. But they study and evaluate these factors solely from the perspective of whether they are conducive to or hinder economic growth.

Such views may also be described as racist, since they are rooted in a profound disrespect for indigenous peoples, for whom the implementation of these views leads to cultural and physical genocide. The governor of Roirama, for example, concluded that the Yanomanis' cultural values and systems were "holding back development" – and that was intolerable for him. Development and economic growth count for more than people.

A consultation on the churches' response to racism organized by the WCC in the Netherlands in 1980 condemned this line of thinking in no uncertain terms:

This system is racist in a variety of ways: it sets the framework for a world order based on the values and interests of the white order; it was historically based substantially on the exploitation of the non-white peoples; it projects a continued and expanding exploitation of the land and resources of eastern and southern hemispheres – regions where the indigenous people are black, brown, red or yellow. In continuing to strip these people from their resources, this system perpetuates their underdevelopment and frustrates their aspirations for the future.

This system is repugnant to the Christian concept of justice, a denial of the lordship of Christ and therefore an abomination to the Creator.

Some believe that indigenous peoples should make a serious effort to integrate themselves into the "mainstream" in order to avoid disintegration and exclusion. Some, mostly non-indigenous persons, would go so far as to say that sharing in a common economic destiny rather than creating a separate indigenous economy is central to the aspirations of indigenous peoples.

Such statements illustrate the paternalism and triumphalism which often characterize those who give primacy to economic growth and development. In the name of realism ("if you can't beat them, join them"), indigenous peoples are urged to "join the club". To the extent that this line of reasoning acknowledges existing discriminatory barriers to indigenous participation in mainstream economic life, it may have some merits. Indigenous people's incomes are significantly lower, unemployment markedly higher and access to capital and bank loans extremely difficult. However, arguments like these can also be a veil for efforts to break indigenous resistance and to lure them (and especially their resources) into the market economy. Assimilation, integration and forced inclusion can in fact lead to disintegration and exclusion.

The choice should not be between integration and exclusion. The only responsible answer is self-determination. Indigenous peoples should have a real choice to "assimilate" or "integrate" or not. Some may chose to "integrate" while others may prefer to keep their own identity and styles of life.

Indigenous businesses

Half of all the indigenous people in the US live below the poverty line, 40 percent of them in housing which a US Senate report has described as "overcrowded and physically deficient". About 40 percent of the adult Indians on the 300 reservations in the US are out of work. Alcoholism and suicide are far above the national averages.

Overall government spending to support Indian causes doubled from US$3 billion to $6 billion between 1985 and 1995. Although some results have been evident – suicides have dropped by 25 percent since 1973 and alcohol-related deaths have been cut by a third in the past 15 years – it is now being argued along neo-liberal lines that rather than increased financial support, Indians should be helped to be more independent and generate their own income.

Some tribes have already put this into practice. The Oklahoma Cherokee raised the proportion of their funds that came from commercial ventures from 10 percent in 1975 to 42 percent in 1986. The Passamaquoddy in Maine invested the $87 million they received in compensation for broken promises over land in the 18th century in a cement plant and other enterprises. The tiny Mashantucket Pequot tribe of 350 members, living in Connecticut, has been especially successful. They run Foxwoods Resort, said to be one of the world's most successful casinos, with annual revenues estimated at nearly $1 billion. While every member of the tribe is guaranteed housing and education, money is distributed on an incentive basis, with points awarded for going to college or for taking part in tribal government.

The Oneida in Wisconsin have used revenues from a slot-machine complex to build a large new factory for the production of electronic components. The tribe already runs an industrial park, a printing firm, a bank, a hotel, and four special Oneida convenience stores. The general quality of life is also improved through spending on subsidized housing, health care, student counselling, a day-care centre and a new elementary school built in the shape of a turtle, a sacred creature in Oneida mythology. In 1995, the Oneida also spent an estimated $11 million recovering land it once owned and reabsorbing it into the tax-free boundaries of its reservation. Nationwide, revenue generated by Indian gambling companies was $58 billion in 1993.

The First Nations in Alaska own considerably more land than their counterparts in the other states of the USA thanks to the 1971 Alaska Native Claims Settlement Act, by which the federal government ceded almost $1 billion in cash and 18 million hectares of land rich with trees, minerals, fish and oil to the state's American Indians. The assets were spread among 12 regional corporations and 200 smaller village companies. Anyone who could claim at least a quarter Inuit (Eskimo), Indian or Aleut blood could receive 100 shares in one of these corporations. The shares can be traded only within the clan and cannot be sold to outsiders. Such a settlement was possible because the indigenous peoples were bargaining from a position of strength. Since 1959, when Alaska became a state, they had organized themselves to fight takeovers of their land and to have a say in how Alaska split its vast territory with the federal government.

The arrangement has caused divisions within the Alaskan Indian communities between those whose companies pursue irresponsible logging operations and those who give priority to the preservation of nature, and between those who want to develop oil fields and those who want to protect the caribou. Another problem has been that the Alaskan Indians quite suddenly had to learn the ins and outs of modern investing.

Some of the companies had a bumpy start, but virtually all have remained intact, with some scoring notable successes. The small Nana tribal corporation now employs more than a fifth of its 5000 shareholders in mining, oil-related work and tourism. The Sitnasuak Native Corp., which represents the 2400 Alaskan Indians in Nome, has built up a very successful investment portfolio, which generated 20 percent of its operating profit in 1995.

Clearly, the Alaskan Indian companies have provided their owners a measure of economic self-determination. For an outsider, however, it is difficult to discern whether indigenous culture and spirituality influence the policies of the American Indian companies in a way which makes them distinct from any other business enterprise.

While indigenous peoples often take better care of unspoiled land than the "developers" who snatch it from them, there are exceptions. Just as indigenous peoples of previous times were introduced to firearms and alcohol – with disastrous consequences – so some are now discovering another powerful and dangerous force: the market. The Kayapo people of the Xingu basin in Brazil won many allies in their struggle against the building of a hydroelectric dam on the Amazon. The rock star Sting travelled all over the world on their behalf. Now they have a proper reservation and contracts for their wild oils and essences with environmentally friendly companies such as the cosmetic chain The Body Shop. At the same time, however, the Kayapo began to exploit vigorously natural resources such as gold and mahogany. The handsome earnings are often spent by their chiefs on ranches, cars and private airplanes or in discotheques. When the Brazilian government pressed the Kayapo to give up the irresponsible logging, it had to backtrack under the violent protest of the tribe.

The Kayapo are not unique. In 1989, the Guajajara of northeastern Brazil held some government agents hostage in order to press for logging permits. A group of Nambikwara, from Mato Grosso, having cut down all of their own hardwood, began to poach on their neighbours'. One wonders what is more destructive for indigenous spirituality – land expropriation or being integrated in the market economy.

NOTES

[1] See Herman E. Daly and John B. Cobb, Jr, *For the Common Good: Redirecting the Economy Toward Community, the Environment and the Future*, Boston, Beacon Press, 1989, p.116.

[2] Walter Brueggemann, "The Land and our Urban Appetites" (unpublished paper).

[3] Cited in "The Cry for Land", a 1988 pastoral letter of the Catholic bishops of Guatemala, p.6.

[4] "The Land: God's Giving, Our Caring", a study document of the American Lutheran Church, 1982.

[5] See *Lutheran World Information*, no.34, 1992.

[6] See Nicholas Dennys, "Invisible Gold: The Vulnerability of Russia's Indigenous People and Forests", *Land and Liberty*, Sept.-Oct. 1993.

[7] *The Catalyst*, Vol. 19, no.5, Sept. 1996.

[8] Quoted by Barbara Rogers, in *Race: No Peace Without Justice*.

8. Markets and Economic Growth

The market is undoubtedly a useful instrument in many domains of economic life. Markets and competition promote efficient use of resources, entrepreneurial skills and creativity; and they contribute to material riches. While the collapse of the centrally planned economies in Central and Eastern Europe has clearly shown how government interference can hinder the positive effects of the market mechanism, the resulting euphoria about the free market as a panacea for a host of economic and social problems is nevertheless unrealistic and even dangerous. Let us look at some of the reasons why.

Purchasing power

Markets register only those needs and wants which are expressed through purchasing power. The basic needs of poor people who do not have enough money to express these needs in the market are ignored. This explains why countries where people are hungry can still export food. Malaria offers another example. Celebrities wear no ribbons to show concern about it; charities hardly mention it in their fund-raising materials. Yet malaria kills far more people each year than AIDS or landmines or scores of other diseases. Around half a billion people catch malaria every year, of whom 2.5 million or so die, more than two-thirds of them children. Ninety percent of malaria victims live in Sub-Saharan Africa. The numbers are increasing as the disease spreads and grows more resistant to existing drugs.

Given these facts, one would expect pharmaceutical companies to be scrambling to develop new, cheap and effective medicines against malaria. But while a number of pills are made for well-to-do visitors to malarial regions, these are far too expensive for those most at risk, the inhabitants of these regions. Research into malaria receives only some US$60 million a year, compared to $140 million for asthma, $300 million for Alzheimer's disease, and $950 million for AIDS.[1] Most of the research on new anti-malaria drugs is done by governments or charities. While the pharmaceutical industry's budget for this type of research is small and steadily declining, research on anti-AIDS drugs has ballooned as AIDS is now the leading cause of death for adults under 45 in Europe and North America.

The conclusion is obvious: because most of the victims of malaria are too poor to pay for the necessary drugs, the market ignores their needs. In rich countries money can be found to pay for expensive anti-AIDS drugs, and it is thus more profitable to focus research on that problem. The situation could of course change if the world's climate continues to warm and malaria were to return to the wealthy North, which it left only a century ago. Pharmaceutical companies might take an interest in such an "emerging market".

Most economists would agree that the market mechanism works best, from an economic point of view, if markets are free. However, very few markets are really free, and most suffer from distortions other than government interventions. We noted earlier that one-third of world trade takes place within individual TNCs, and that the prices in these intra-firm transactions have very little to do with market prices. Monopoly power can also lead to gross market distortions which destroy most of the positive effects which markets can bring.

Markets and ethics

Markets used to be human places, used not only to exchange goods and services, but also for people to meet and to communicate. There are still markets which also fulfil such a social function. In Kenya, for example, the *Sokoni* (people's market) is a place where news is exchanged and discussed. But in recent years a more Western-style market, the *Nduka*, has developed alongside the *Sokoni*, providing for much less opportunity for social interaction.

In the course of time, transactions in the market have become increasingly impersonal, and producers and consumers have become more and more detached from each other. Rarely do we know who produced the goods we buy in the supermarket or under what conditions. As a result, the moral obligations implicit in community life are obscured, reducing people's sense of responsibility for their behaviour in the marketplace. While many markets promote material prosperity, they tend to undermine a sense of responsibility.

The well-known advocates of the free market Milton and Rose Friedman have written that "no society... has ever achieved prosperity and freedom unless voluntary exchange has been its dominant principle of organization".[2] While this may be true, it must be realized that free markets promote a particular kind of freedom – the freedom to act as one wills without having to ask permission from others. This individualized concept of freedom neglects that human beings can be truly human only in community. The Friedmans' insight is useful only if it is restricted to a well-defined, tightly circumscribed sphere of life. In today's society the market and its logic, rather than being contained, have penetrated almost all spheres of life.

Whereas market transactions were once embedded in a wider web of social relationships, the tendency today is for social relationships to become embedded in and often conditional on the pervasive forces of the market. More and more aspects of life can be bought and sold. They have become "commodified". Things once considered sacred are now becoming objects of market transactions. Poor people in Brazil sell their blood – more of it than is healthy – to blood banks to get some money. In India a grisly but profitable market for human organs has developed. Shady organizations procure kidneys from the poor to sell to the rich. The rich pay about US$7000 for such a transplant while the poor donor may receive as little as $160.[3]

For a handsome fee, surrogate mothers carry a child for somebody else, thus creating a market for reproductive services. In the US the bill for this can be up to $65,000. As can be expected, there is competition on the baby-market: a Russian agency offers surrogacy services for $25,000. And where there are markets and competition, there is also advertising: on Internet a prospective surrogate mother specifies that she has blonde hair, green eyes and is of Caucasian complexion.

Churches have not escaped the influence of the market. The impressive commercial empires built up by televangelists in the USA are well-known; and many of them have exported their "product" to other countries. But the "logic of the market" is more widely applied to churches. During the controversy in the Church of England over the ordination of women to the priesthood, *The Economist* suggested in an editorial that the church should split over this issue: "Schism is healthy for churches... It is also healthy for congregations, for the best free-market reason: it allows them more choice."

Evaluating everything from the perspective of the logic of the market leads to judgments which can only be described as perverse. Some years ago, a chief economist with the World Bank wrote a memo asking whether the Bank should not be encouraging the migration of "dirty" industries to the least developed countries, which are, according to the memo, vastly under-polluted. Concern over an agent that causes a small increase in the odds of contracting prostate cancer will obviously be much lower in a country where the mortality rate is already very high. The memo argued that the costs of health-impairing pollution depend on the lost earnings from increased morbidity and mortality. From this point of view, it is most advantageous that health-impairing pollution be concentrated in countries where the wages are lowest. The lives of poor people are worth less than those of the rich. The memo concluded that the economic logic behind dumping a load of toxic waste in the poorest country is impeccable.[4]

A 1995 report by a working group – mostly economists from the OECD countries – of the Intergovernmental Panel on Climate Change calculated that global warming would lead to a loss of 1.5 to 2 percent of the global gross domestic product by the year 2050. One of the main conclusions of the report was that the industrialized North would suffer 66 percent of the total damage done by climate change while the non-OECD countries would incur only about a third. The main reason for this surprising conclusion was that, according to the method used by the working group, a human life was valued at \$1.5 million in the OECD countries and \$100,000 in the rest of the world.[5]

Considering the market a useful instrument is different from seeing it as an infallible compass pointing the way to a better future. Markets must work for people, not people for markets. They must be regulated by political and social forces to ensure that their negative effects are kept under control. The necessary measures include effective anti-monopoly legislation, consumer protection, labour legislation to ensure good working conditions, social safety nets to protect vulnerable groups and environmental protection.

At another level, restraining the all-pervasive nature of the "market logic" is basically a spiritual and cultural challenge. To go against the "market logic" requires an attitude of cultural disobedience which may be even more difficult than civil disobedience. A society which is a grand auction block, where even sacred things like human lives can be bought and sold and values are replaced by prices, is a chilling reminder of the vision of the Apocalypse (Rev. 18:3).

Economic growth

Maximizing economic growth has become the central long-term economic policy objective almost all over the world. This is a relatively new phenomenon, arising from the advent and spread of capitalism, which requires economic growth. Economic growth is seen as the chief indicator of economic success, and politicians generally make it a key theme of election campaigns, often accompanied by the promise that this growth will combat unemployment.

When economic growth becomes the centrepiece of economic policies, economics as a science is reduced to promoting the efficient allocation of production factors. Progress, success, welfare and development are measured entirely apart from considerations of distribution or environmental consequences – and if there are problems with distribution or environmental destruction, economic growth is seen as necessary to solve these. Thus welfare states are being dismantled in Western Europe at a time when the continent has never before been so rich. To keep even the basic elements of a social safety net, it is argued, more economic growth is necessary. If too many cars are causing traffic jams, the only solution is to build more roads.

This is not to suggest that economic growth is never welcome. On the contrary, the fact that millions of people live in dire poverty and that the world's population is still growing means that a certain economic growth is absolutely necessary to enable employment, income and a decent human life. Some countries in the South have managed to combine economic growth with the reduction of poverty, though not always with a narrowing of the gap between rich and poor.

Economic growth has brought many benefits. Indeed, as a WCC study document says, the production of goods can be a blessing, as the word "good" in fact suggests.[6] But economic growth needs to be qualified. Growth for growth's sake is – in the words of the WCC's seventh assembly – the strategy of the cancer cell.

The sustained economic growth the world has experienced since the second world war has been accompanied by a growing gap between rich and poor, both globally and within most countries. The benefits of this type of growth do not automatically "trickle down" to the poor, and this is not the type of growth that they need. At the same time, this growth has gone hand in hand with continued environmental destruction and depletion of natural resources.

The economic deprivation and ecological degradation which characterize unqualified economic growth are in fact two sides of the same coin. This is reflected in the disproportionate ways in which poor people suffer from environmental destruction. Often they live close to polluted areas, in inadequate housing with poor sanitation; as peasants they often possess poor, degraded and arid land; as landless agricultural workers they often have to work with toxic insecticides, pesticides and herbicides; their health is often endangered by polluted drinking water and fishing water. Poor women have extra burdens as they have to walk longer distances to find clean water and wood for fuel.

Poverty is polluting, just as overconsumption is. To survive, poor people often have little choice but to overuse and destroy their natural environment. This, in turn, aggravates poverty. Poor peasants may well know that they are damaging the environment when they cut down trees and bushes, but they have little choice if they are to feed their children. In poor societies, what is at risk is not the quality of life but life itself. Combatting poverty is thus as important a requirement for safeguarding the environment as promoting less wasteful consumption by those who are materially better off.

The question is thus what kind of economic growth is necessary to save lives and improve the quality of life. This implies that certain types of growth need to be promoted while limits have to be put on destructive economic growth which leads to greater inequities and undermines life-support systems.

As a sub-system of the larger eco-system, the economy cannot grow beyond the limits of the system of which it is a part. The limited carrying capacity of the earth cannot endure an ever-expanding production of the kind of goods which require finite resources and energy and destroy the environment. A 3 percent growth rate may sound modest on the face of it, but it implies a doubling of production and consumption every 25 years. Even taking technological progress into account, certain types of growth simply cannot continue. Setting limits to growth will require intervention in the market and that will lead to opposition. However, as a WCC report observes, it would not be the first time the world community has found it necessary to impose limits. Slave-owners vigorously opposed the abolition of slavery on economic grounds; few would today argue that slavery should be reinstated.[7]

The need to set limits is clear when we consider that
- non-renewable resources such as minerals and fossil fuels are being exhausted;
- renewable resources such as fisheries and forests are being over-exploited, leading to loss of topsoil, erosion and floods;
- health is at risk through water and air pollution;

– accelerated climate change is threatening lives and livelihoods;[8]
– bio-diversity and the number of species are quickly diminishing.

All these processes have economic consequences. Global agricultural losses from desertification, for example, have been estimated at around $26 billion per year. The effect of the prevailing pattern of unqualified economic growth is the colonization of the biosphere and of the future. It is inherently unsustainable.

Imposing limits and intervening in the market can take two basic forms. One is an outright ban on certain products such as hazardous chemicals. The second policy alternative is to steer the economy into the direction of more justice, peace and ecological health. Such policies could include the following measures:

1. Poverty and inequity must be combatted, as these are responsible for a significant share of environmental pollution; while the life-styles and consumption patterns of well-to-do people need to become more responsible. Among the preconditions for the fight against poverty and inequity are the cancellation of the foreign debt of the poorest countries and the establishment of a more equitable global trading system.

2. Population growth needs to be addressed. According to the United Nations Fund for Population Activities, the world's population will double from 5.4 billion in 1991 to 10 billion in 2050, with some 95 percent of the additional people being born in the South. But it must be added immediately that the strain on the environment and material resources caused by population growth is much greater in the North: an average person in the North uses about ten times as many material resources as an average Southerner, and the wealthiest 25 percent of the world's population accounts for about three-quarters of the total greenhouse gas emissions which lead to climate change. Therefore, the issue of population growth requires a balanced approach.

3. Fiscal policies can steer economies in the right direction even in an era of globalization, especially if coordinated

at the regional and global levels. "Eco-taxes" could impose higher levies on non-renewable energy resources and products that are especially polluting while introducing a milder fiscal regime for goods produced in an environmentally friendly way. A TNC based in the Netherlands has made the interesting proposal of replacing value-added taxes (VAT) by a more ecologically and actuarially correct levy termed "value-extracted taxes" (VET). A part of the revenue raised by such taxes could be used to stimulate technological research and experiments for the sustainable use of resources.[9]

4. Production and consumption activities may have unintended consequences – positive or negative – for others. A beekeeper's bees may benefit the owners of nearby orchards, while smoke from a factory may have adverse effects on people living in the neighbourhood. These unintended side effects are not accounted for in the market. The beekeeper cannot charge for the services of his bees, nor are people compensated for living in a smoky environment. Yet, the effects are very real.[10] One way to deal with this issue is the principle "the polluter pays". The purchase price of nuclear electricity, for example, should include the costs of waste storage for the necessary thousands of years. Applying this principle will stimulate efficiency, since firms required to internalize their pollution costs will try to minimize their use of energy and production of waste.

Gross national product

Calculating the real costs and benefits of production is not easy. This becomes apparent when we look at the most commonly used indicator to measure economic growth. Typically, a nation's economic performance is measured by its gross domestic product (GDP) and gross national product (GNP). The former is the total value, in money terms, of all the production in a country in one year. The GNP is the GDP corrected for payments from and to people in other countries.

As measures of the flow of money, GNP and GDP are valid instruments, but as measures of value and of quality of life they are much more problematic. A major flaw is that they count only goods and services exchanged for money. Work which is not paid for is not measured. If I bring my car to the garage to have it fixed, this is added to the GDP; if I manage to repair it myself, it is not registered, although the end result – a functioning car – is the same. Since most unpaid work is done at home, and since it is still done primarily by women, their work is under-represented in the statistics. Volunteer charity and community work are also excluded from the statistics, since no money changes hands. Activities vital to the health and cohesion of a society thus go unrecorded, creating the false impression that these are irrelevant to the wealth of a country.

GDP and GNP lump together good things and bad things indiscriminately. A dollar spent on care for children or the elderly has the same weight in the statistics as a dollar spent on the manufacture of landmines. Environmental degradation, pollution and resource depletion fall outside of the scope of GDP and GNP. If a person is badly injured in an automobile accident and becomes an invalid for the rest of his or her life, this loss is not subtracted from the GNP or GDP. But the charge to tow away the car, the hospital bills, the price of the wheelchair are all *added* to the GDP. The more car accidents, the more economic growth! As Chilean economist Manfred Max-Neef has observed:

> The GNP... is based on an arithmetic that would be unacceptable on page 1 of the simplest arithmetic books in elementary school: the only sign that exists is plus; you can only add, never subtract. So any process that generates a monetary flux or a market transaction is acceptable. It is totally irrelevant whether it is productive, unproductive, or destructive – it all adds to the GNP.[11]

Parts of the national accounts statistics are thus based on double counting. Environmental losses as a result of economic activities are not written off as costs; instead, both the activity itself and the price of the cleanup are included in the statistics. If a forest is cut down, the value of the timber is added to the GNP, but no account is taken of the loss of the benefits previously derived from the existence of the forest.

While the gross national product increases, the gross *natural* product diminishes.

Alternative indicators

Despite the evident distortions which make GNP and GDP dubious as pictures of reality and dangerous as guides for economic policy, they continue to be used, in part because it is so difficult to develop workable alternatives. How can one calculate the value of domestic activities or the life of somebody who dies in an accident or of a disease or a rainforest which is cleared or a species which becomes extinct?

While it may be impossible to find one single alternative to GNP and GDP, using a set of new indicators may provide a better picture of what constitutes improvement in the quality of life. One organization which has tried to develop social and environmental indicators to measure progress is the New Economics Foundation. Other well-known forums for reflecting about these issues are The Other Economic Summit (TOES) and the Living Economy Network. Efforts to develop a "green national product" resulted in an Index of Sustainable Economic Welfare, which takes account of issues like income distribution, environmental damage, the value of housework and resource depletion.[12]

Perhaps the best-known effort is the Human Development Index (HDI) of the United Nations Development Programme (UNDP). Since 1990 this list has annually ranked 174 countries by a measurement that takes account of such factors as life expectancy, educational attainment and basic purchasing power. The UNDP also publishes a Gender-Related Development Index, which attempts to adjust the HDI for gender inequality.

The HDI ranking of countries may differ significantly from their ranking by real GDP per capita. In recent years countries like Costa Rica, Vietnam and Cuba have enjoyed a better quality of life (as measured by the HDI) than their GDP ranking would suggest. Other countries have a high GDP per person but a relatively low HDI ranking. Hong

Kong, for example, has the sixth largest GDP per person in the world but was only 22nd on the HDI list in 1996.

Although the annual publication of the HDI has improved the understanding of progress in the quality of life, alternative measurements have also elicited resistance. For example, when the World Summit for Social Development (Copenhagen 1995) recommended including unremunerated productive work in national statistics in order to give a better picture of a nation's wealth, some Southern countries objected, fearing that this could make them look rather rich and thus reduce their chances to qualify for foreign aid!

A spiritual challenge

Statistics, like economics, are never neutral or value-free. They incorporate worldviews, goals and social values. The standard indicators for measuring economic growth or the wealth of nations reveal the hierarchy of values of those who use them: we measure what we treasure.

If improving the quality of life is the goal, we must avoid being misled by the obsession to maximize unqualified economic growth – which is rather like supposing that the quality of a symphony improves when more notes are added. If economic growth alone has proved to be no solution for the twin crisis of environmental and economic degradation, why not consider whether successful implementation of policies for poverty removal, long-term employment generation, and environmental restoration will have GNP growth as a side-effect, rather than following the evidently false assumption that benefits of economic growth automatically trickle down to serve those who need them most? Instead of beginning with economies and their growth, what would it mean to start with communities and their well being?[13] Such an alternative approach would require, from the outset, the active participation in decision-making processes of those who are affected by the decisions. It would be a "building up" rather than a "trickle down" approach, starting with the needs of local communities and using these as the basis for national and global policies.

There are spiritual as well as material limits to unqualified growth. The WCC study document *Christian Faith and the World Economy Today* observes that ever-increasing production can paradoxically lead to scarcity rather than abundance. Goods like clean air, clean water, stillness and time become more and more scarce. The "unpriced scarcity" of these so-called non-economic goods is growing because human needs and desires are increasing faster than we can meet them. If human desires are assumed to be virtually limitless, scarcity increases regardless of the current level of material prosperity, because people are never satisfied and always want more. Many seem to have lost the idea of having "enough", even though one cannot be aware of abundance without having an awareness of what is "enough" – because abundance is by definition *more than* enough.

Of course, as Larry Rasmussen writes, for millions of destitute people, to *have* more is required in order to *be* more. But once people are above the poverty line, there is very little correlation of happiness and well-being with increased consumption and rising incomes. Satisfactions in life relate more closely to the quality of family life and friendships, work, leisure and spiritual richness. None of these is well measured by the GDP. In fact, in societies with the highest levels of consumption, where the basic choice of serving God or mammon has been faced squarely and decided in favour of the latter, there seems to be vast psychological and spiritual emptiness.[14] People who have lived under communist regimes have sometimes been asked how difficult it was to be a Christian under such circumstances. It is equally pertinent to pose this same question to those living in contemporary consumer societies. To go against the tide requires considerable spiritual strength and is perhaps the greatest challenge to churches and Christians who wish to keep the faith in today's global economy.

NOTES

1 *The Economist*, 23 Aug. 1997.
2 Milton and Rose Friedman, *Free to Choose*, New York, Avon, 1980, p.3.
3 *International Herald Tribune*, 5 May 1995.
4 *The Economist*, 8 Feb. 1992.
5 Chakravarthi Raghavan, "Southern Lives Are Cheaper, Say Climate Change Economists", *Third World Resurgence*, no. 64.
6 *Christian Faith and the World Economy Today*, p.30.
7 On the limits to growth see for example John B. Cobb, Jr, *Sustainability: Economics, Ecology and Justice*, Maryknoll NY, Orbis, 1992; Paul Ekins, ed, *The Living Economy: A New Economics in the Making*, London and New York, Routledge & Kegan Paul, 1986; *Sustainable Growth: A Contradiction in Terms*, Geneva, The Visser 't Hooft Endowment Fund for Leadership Development, 1993.
8 See *Accelerated Climate Change: Sign of Peril, Test of Faith*, a study paper from the World Council of Churches, Geneva, WCC, 1994.
9 Hazel Henderson, "Changing Paradigms and Indicators: Implementing Equitable, Sustainable and Participatory Development", in Griesgraber and Gunter, eds, *Development: New Paradigms and Principles*, p.124.
10 Donald Hay, *Economics Today: A Christian Critique*, Leicester, Inter-Varsity Press, 1989, p.286.
11 Cited in Clifford W. Cobb and John B. Cobb, Jr, *The Green National Product: A Proposed Index of Sustainable Economic Welfare*, Lanham MD, University Press of America, 1994, p.19.
12 See Victor Anderson, *Alternative Economic Indicators*, London and New York, Routledge & Kegan Paul, 1991; Paul Ekins and Manfred Max-Neef, eds, *Real-Life Economics: Understanding Wealth Creation*, London and New York, Routledge & Kegan Paul, 1992; Herman E. Daly and John B. Cobb, Jr, *For the Common Good*.
13 Larry L. Rasmussen, "Sustainable Development and Sustainable Community: Divergent Paths", in *Development Assessed: Ecumenical Reflections and Actions on Development*, Geneva, WCC, 1995.
14 Larry L. Rasmussen, *Earth Community, Earth Ethics*, Geneva, WCC, 1996, p.149.

9. Sabbath and Jubilee

The sabbath, sabbath year and jubilee year offer a powerful vision for Jews and Christians reflecting about economic issues. Obviously, the texts on these topics in the Hebrew Bible cannot serve as prescriptions for modern economic life, but we can try to discern and follow the core elements of the biblical message.

The sabbath is the seventh day of the week. According to the first creation account in Genesis, "God blessed the seventh day and hallowed it, because on it God rested from all the work that he had done in creation" (Gen. 2:3). The ten commandments, into which the law of sabbath is incorporated, are recorded in Exodus 20 and Deuteronomy 5, though with differing texts at this point. Exodus emphasizes that observing the sabbath means following the example of God, who ceased to work when creation had been finished. This can be called the *theological* motive of the sabbath: we recall that God is the Creator of all things, and like God we have to cease work on the seventh day. Deuteronomy 5:15 gives another reason: "Remember that you were a slave in the land of Egypt, and the Lord your God brought you out from there with a mighty hand and an outstretched arm; therefore the Lord your God commanded you to keep the sabbath day." This *social* motive puts the sabbath in the context of the Exodus, the liberation from slavery. In a sense, perhaps, stopping work at regular intervals liberates us from slavery. In any case, observing the sabbath implies remembering and celebrating with gratitude God's liberating power in history.

Several chapters later the book of Exodus refers to the sabbath year:

> For six years you shall sow your land and gather in its yield; but the seventh year you shall let it rest and lie fallow, so that the poor of your people may eat; and what they leave the wild animals may eat. You shall do the same with your vineyard and your olive orchard (Ex. 23:10-12; cf. Lev. 25:2-7).

Three elements emerge from a reading of this text. The first is the evident concern for the poor who can share in the fruits and produce of the land. The second is an agricultural and possibly ecological element. Yehuda Feliks points out that a field left fallow for a year would produce double the crop the next season. Jewish farmers thus obtained much larger harvests than farmers in other countries; and they were later praised for this by Roman agricultural engineers.[1] There are several problems with this interpretation. One is that there are indications that the peoples around Israel also practised land rotation, so that this was nothing exceptional. Moreover, while the Exodus text permits land rotation – one piece would lie fallow, another would be sown – the corresponding passage in Leviticus implies a universal fallow year for all fields simultaneously every seven years. This would have caused hardship and would hardly elicit the praise of Roman agricultural experts. Finally, if fallow land is to produce extra crop the next season, it must be ploughed. Reference to the land producing sufficient food for the fallow year implies that it could not be ploughed. Feliks suggests that the Israelites may have followed the Exodus text but did not fully implement the Leviticus text because it was impractical.

The third element regarding the institution of the fallow year was the recognition that the land belongs to God. The other peoples surrounding Israel let land lie fallow in order to appease the gods of the land; Israel adopted the custom and gave it a new interpretation: Yahweh is the owner of the land (Ps. 24:1) who gives it in grace to all Israel. The people of Israel can use, but not misuse it. Every seven years they have to cease tilling the land. Working with something that belongs to God requires a respectful attitude.

Connected with the fallow year is the release of debts as legislated in Deuteronomy:

> Every seventh year you shall grant a remission of debts. And this is the manner of the remission: every creditor shall remit the claim that is held against a neighbour, not exacting it of a neighbour who is a member of the community, because the Lord's remission has been proclaimed. Of a foreigner you may exact it, but you must remit your claim on whatever any mem-

ber of your community owes you. There will, however, be no one in need among you... if only you will obey the Lord your God by diligently observing this entire commandment (Deut. 15:1-5).

The same chapter refers to the release of slaves:

If a member of your community, whether a Hebrew man or a Hebrew woman, is sold to you and works for you six years, in the seventh year you shall set that person free (12-13).

Some scholars consider that this latter text is here only by coincidence. Slaves could be held for only six years and the year of this release need not necessarily be a sabbath year.[2] Debt remittance was also practised in neighbouring countries. During their first year of reign, Mesopotamian kings often cancelled debts, released slaves and returned land seized by creditors. But what Deuteronomy envisages is not an act of charity by a secular king, but a religious institution to obey the heavenly Redeemer. Regarding the release of slaves, the Deuteronomy text says: "Remember that you were a slave in the land of Egypt, and the Lord your God redeemed you" (Deut. 15:15). God's grace and liberating power set an example for humans to follow.

Because there was a debt release in each sabbath year, it would only be human nature for people to stop giving loans or at least attach very harsh conditions to them when the sabbath year was near, for who would want to lose his or her money? The Deuteronomy passage foresees this (vv. 6-12), but rather than legislating that loans should continue to be given, it appeals to the faith of the Israelites, urging them to be charitable, to go beyond the letter of the law, and promising them God's blessings. The inclination to follow the "logic of the market" was to be resisted.

Nevertheless, ways were found to get around the debt release. Rabbi Hillel, a contemporary of Jesus, created the *prosbul* provision, by which the creditor and debtor agreed that the loan would be repaid despite the intervention of the sabbath year. It was argued that this benefited both the creditors, since it secured their loans, and the borrowers, since it enabled them to bridge the period during which credits were likely to dry up.[3]

This line of reasoning sounds familiar; indeed, in the context of the contemporary debt crisis the argument is often heard that debt cancellation would in fact hurt poor countries by depriving them of future loans from creditors who had lost faith in their capacity to repay. The *prosbul* is an example of the contextualization of the Torah, instituted because people were not in fact lending when the sabbath year approached, thus going against the Deuteronomy prescription. This circumvention could only take place, as Raphael Jospe argues, because the authority for the sabbatical year had become rabbinic rather than biblical.[4] Hillel's concern may have been primarily for the poor, but the *prosbul* compromised an important idea – that debts should last only for a short period of time and not for a lifetime. The sabbath year prescription for debt release was aimed to prevent debt bondage and the accompanying horrible results such as described in Job: "There are those who snatch the orphan child from the breast, and take as a pledge the infant of the poor" (Job 24:9; see also 2 Kings 4:1; Neh. 5:1-5). It is unclear how the *prosbul* could prevent such situations. In any case, poor people in the debt-ridden countries of the South will understand the outcry of Job.

Inability to repay a loan often resulted in slavery. Jewish exegetes insist that there was no true slavery in Israel, certainly not the politically entrenched form of slavery which was indispensable to the organization of the state in ancient Greece or Rome. The Hebrew word *ebed*, sometimes translated as slave, usually implies nothing more than one who renders some service to another. An *ebed* had to be treated fairly. He could marry the owner's daughter and get the inheritance if the owner had no son (Gen. 15:3), or perhaps even if there was a son, as Sarah feared (Gen. 21:10). When an *ebed* was set free, he should not go empty-handed: "Provide liberally out of your flock, your threshing floor and your winepress, thus giving to him some of the bounty with which the Lord your God has blessed you" (Deut.15-14). The former *ebed* should be able to make a new beginning, lest he become an *ebed* again. Some even preferred to remain with their owner when they had the right to leave (Deut. 15:16). Robert North states that in an unpoliced tribal society like Israel, it was in some ways a worse evil to be "unattached" than to be a serf or a slave.[5] It is not difficult to see the analogy here to the growing number of people in today's world who are excluded rather than exploited.

Regulations regarding usury or interest are not part of the institution of the sabbath year. The earliest biblical allusions to lending money are those which encourage it as an expression of charity and without tolerating usury or interest (Ex. 22:25; Deut. 23:20; Lev. 25:36). North argues that the different texts about charging interest are ambiguous and notes that Jesus in one of his parables spoke non-committally of the prevailing practice of charging interest (Matt. 25:27). Most likely, the intention was that charging interest was prohibited only on a loan made to a Jew who was poor (Ex. 22:25).

Most references in the Hebrew Bible to lending refer to loans for survival, not for venture capital aimed at making profits. Characteristically, collateral for survival loans were the land, animals, agricultural equipment or indentured labour of the members of the household of the poor. Again there is an overriding concern for the poor. If a poor man gives his cloak as pledge, the creditor should give it back to him at sunset so he can use it at night (Deut. 24:12-14). The provision that the next-of-kin should act as redeemer of land or family members foreclosed upon when serving as a collateral (cf. Ruth 4:1-12) is a clear sign of responsibility in community.

The jubilee vision

The jubilee legislation (Lev. 25:1-55; 27:16-24) rests on the same foundations as the sabbath year. Every fiftieth year the land is to lie fallow and the Hebrew slaves are set free. In addition, a new feature appears: all property reverts to the original owner who, because of poverty, had been obliged to sell it during the previous period.

Land may be sold but not in perpetuity, "because the land is mine" (Lev. 25:23); and if land is sold, the purchase price should be regulated according to the number of years still to go until the jubilee year (vv. 14-16). Theoretically, then, the land was only lent to the "buyer"; at the jubilee it returned to the original owner. An exception was made for house property in a walled city (vv. 29f.), which fell under old Canaanite law, based on private ownership. In this sense, the economy in Israel was a dual economy – as was the case in colonized countries until the middle of the 20th century and still is in regions where indigenous peoples live. Further exceptions were granted to the Levites, reflecting their special position as the priestly class in ancient Israel.

Whether the jubilee year was ever put into practice is doubtful, and how it would have functioned has been the subject of extensive debate. What is more important is to try to discern what motivated this extraordinary piece of social legislation, what its central elements are and what this may mean for today.

The overwhelming impression one gets from reading the institutions for the sabbath, sabbath year and jubilee year is that God is a God of grace. To follow God is to enact this grace and justice for the poor in daily life and in the institutions that govern society. As Yahweh led the Israelites out of slavery, they should beware of making slaves of each other. As the land belongs to God who gives it to people to use, the people should treat it with respect. As God is the Creator of all things, including time, people should at regular intervals cease to work in order to bless God. As God is the Redeemer of all, loans which place poor people in debt bondage should be redeemed. All these institutions are one great training in gratitude for God's amazing grace.

The overriding concern is for the poor. The fallow year was instituted to provide food for the poor (Ex. 23:11): justice is the fruit of rest for the land – an insight indigenous peoples will recognize. Poverty next to wealth leads to the fragmentation of society. This may explain the emphasis put on the family and the community. Family holdings of land were inalienable. The next-of-kin had the responsibility to redeem family members if necessary. The first concern was for human need, not for private ownership, maximizing profits or following the "natural law" of the market – a powerful message for today's world in which the gap between rich and poor is growing and societies seem to consist of aggregations of competing individuals rather than closely-knit communities based on solidarity and care. In this context, the link between the jubilee year and Pentecost, which Christians celebrate 50 days after Easter, is interesting. According to Acts 2, after the Holy Spirit was poured out, "all who believed were together and had all things in common; they would sell their possessions and goods and distribute the proceeds to all, as any had need" (Acts 2:44-46). Acts 4 goes on to say that "great grace was upon them all. There was not a needy person among them" (Acts 4:33-34).

The sabbath and jubilee institutions are about the restoration of the people of Israel, who are invited to come home, to restore their *oikos*. Placed in the context of liturgy and worship, these institutions reveal a deeply religious concept of justice and equality. Konrad Raiser reminds us that the jubilee year is proclaimed through the sound of the trumpet on the day of atonement. Therefore, the whole jubilee legislation can be interpreted as an example of the "liturgy after the liturgy". This echoes the prophetic witness about true worship (Isa. 58) which Jesus affirms in his teaching about the sabbath (Mark 2). The church fathers interpreted the jubilee in the light of the resurrection and the outpouring of the Spirit as the manifestation of the time of salvation, of the fullness of life offered by God. This could lead to a new reflection about efforts to reconstruct human community.[6]

The institution of the jubilee year can also be seen in messianic terms: it points to the era of liberty, peace and prosperity when the Messiah comes. In his first sermon in Nazareth, Jesus proclaims this liberty by quoting Isaiah 61 (Luke 4:18-19). The Lord's prayer taught by Jesus becomes a jubilee prayer when we pray: "Forgive us our debts as we forgive those who are indebted to us."

This messianic hope is an inspiration for those who go against the tide and who do not want to give up. It is a reminder that the status quo is temporary and calls for imagination in looking for solutions to the problems of today. In a time of crass materialism, when so many seem to be obsessed by possessions, the jubilee vision calls for cultural disobedience by putting limits on the frenzy of acquisitiveness. The sabbath, sabbath year and jubilee year emphasize that "to be" is not "to have" but to provide justice to the poor. They resist the logic of the market based on endless accumulation and competition. Over against the right of the strongest, they put the right of the weakest and the poor. Over against the inclination to dominate the earth, they put the notion of dominion and patrimony.

The creation story does not end on the sixth day, the day of multiplication and subduing the earth. The sixth day is followed by the seventh, the day of rest and ceasing to work. Subduing the earth is not a goal in itself but has the sabbath as its limit and its destination. The sabbath is the celebration of the fulfilment of human beings and the whole of creation. The sabbath commandment is in fact an invitation to be human in a creation which is very good. Yet the invitation is conditional: Adam and Eve were not allowed to eat from the tree of the knowledge of good and evil. Why should human beings not know about good and evil? Indeed, how can we make ethical choices without such knowledge? One possible interpretation is that people should know about limits. In the Garden of Eden, in God's good creation, there is plenty to enjoy but we should know where and when to cease. Not everything which is possible is desirable or responsible. Our ethical consciousness is shown when we put limits to the desire to consume more and more.

There are weaknesses in the sabbath year and jubilee year institutions, powerful as their vision of economic justice is. Both call for corrections of the outcome of an unjust political-economic system while leaving the prevailing system intact. Measures which could avoid the need for corrections would be preferable. The sabbath and jubilee year provisions can be seen as a social safety net to prevent things from getting totally out of hand, but what we need is a permanent and systemic restructuring of economic life. The jubilee and sabbath year clearly emphasize a "preferential option for the poor". But how do poor people read the institution of the sabbath day? How can they cease to work if work is a matter of mere survival? Is the sabbath not a luxury for those who can afford it?

In spite of these reservations, the jubilee motif has played an important role in the struggle for justice. It was important in the struggle against slavery, it is being used by churches in Korea in the quest for re-unification of that divided country, it played a role in Indonesia when the country remembered 50 years of independence, and it is a theme used to argue for the cancellation of foreign debts of the heavily indebted countries.[7] The purpose of the sabbath inspired the campaign of churches in the United Kingdom to "Keep Sunday Special" in reaction to government plans to allow shops to be open on Sundays. Churches in other countries have used the same concept to argue for a curb on consumerism.[8] As the WCC assembly in Canberra stated:

> For Jews and Christians together the institutions of the Sabbath, sabbatical year and the jubilee year provide a clear vision on economic and ecological reconciliation, social transformation and personal renewal... Should we not contemplate and revitalize the biblical concept of Sabbath, sabbatical and jubilee year to substitute a global liberation of creation within 50 years for the gloomy future now predicted by ecologists from all over the world?

The WCC eighth assembly in Harare, 1998, organized under the Jubilee-related theme "Turn to God – Rejoice in Hope" is a good occasion to take up these questions.

NOTES

[1] Yehuda Feliks, "Jewish Farmers and the Sabbatical Year", in Hans Ucko, ed., *The Jubilee Challenge*, Geneva, WCC, 1997, pp.165ff.

[2] Robert Gnuse, *You Shall Not Steal: Community and Property in the Biblical Tradition*, Maryknoll NY, Orbis, 1985, p.33.

[3] See Leon Klenicki, "Jewish Understandings of Sabbatical Year and Jubilee", in Ucko, ed., *op. cit.*, pp.41ff.

[4] Raphael Jospe, "Sabbath, Sabbatical and Jubilee: Jewish Ethical Perspectives", in *ibid.*, pp.77ff.

[5] Robert North, *Sociology of the Biblical Jubilee*, Rome, Pontifical Biblical Institute, 1954, p.2.

[6] Konrad Raiser, "What 'Jubilee' Might Mean Today", *Perspectives*, Vol. 11, no.3, March 1996.

[7] See Bill Peters, "An Introduction to the Jubilee 2000 Campaign for International Debt Remission", *Bulletin of the Association of Christian Economists*, no.26, autumn 1995.

[8] C.B. Posthumus Meyes, *Een dag van staken: Zuinig zijn op de zondag*, Zoetermeer NL, Boekencentrum, 1995.

10. Signs of Hope

At the international level one has to look hard for encouraging examples of deliberate and concrete actions which bring more than piecemeal improvements for poor people and the environment. Despite its shortcomings, the HIPC initiative to reduce foreign debt (see p.61 above) is one such step in the right direction. Changes in the policies of the World Bank, aimed at greater transparency, environmental awareness and cooperation with organizations in civil society, should be welcomed. The United Nations' series of conferences on environment, population, social development, gender issues and human rights have produced important declarations and promises though most still wait to be implemented.

Regionally, several noteworthy examples of cooperation beyond mere economic liberalization can be found, of which the European Union is the most advanced example. Yet it too is finding it difficult to convince its citizens that improving social policies is at least as important as promoting economic cooperation.

The scope for independent national policies is generally reduced in the wake of growing globalization, and local initiatives can also hardly avoid the negative effects of this process. Nevertheless, at the level of civil society there are examples of initiatives which go against the tide in seeking to participate in the (global) economy on their own terms and to establish just, participatory and sustainable communities. A few examples of such signs of hope are given in this last chapter. While not downplaying the importance of charity, we shall concentrate here on examples which emphasize self-help and participation.

Fair trade

When people bought goods and services in earlier times, they often knew the producer. The development and spread of international trade has steadily weakened this link between producer and consumer. Not knowing where the goods we purchase come from or the conditions under which they have been produced limits the possibilities for socially and environmentally responsible consumption, making it difficult to apply ethics in everyday economic life.

At the same time, small producers have gained little from expanding conventional international trade. Their percentage of the price paid by the ultimate consumer is negligible compared to what is received by the intermediaries who sell the products to export companies which pass them on to shopping chains in the country of destination. Peruvian asparagus-pickers earn only 0.2 percent of the final price. Wages for Sri Lankan tea plantation workers – whose health, education and housing needs are almost completely neglected – account for only 7 percent of the price paid by the consumer. Brazilian grape workers, who often suffer from pesticide-linked illnesses, get less than 8 US cents per kilo.

To shorten this gap between producers and consumers, Alternative Trade Organizations (ATOs) buy goods directly from small producer groups in the South and sell these through shops, mail order companies, churches and the like. Producers thus have a better chance to realize a fair price for their products and a decent and more secure income. Since the mid-1960s several hundred ATOs have been established, and the retail value of "fair trade" between the South and the North is estimated at US$300-500 million per year.[1] Although this is a small proportion of overall trade flows, it is rising and can be significant in key markets such as coffee. Fair trade has also enhanced awareness of the social and environmental impacts of purchasing decisions, as products often include information about their origin.

Fair trade products are now moving into mainstream outlets such as supermarkets, greatly increasing their potential market shares. In the Netherlands, for example, the Max Havelaar Foundation and others have been successful in introducing fair trade coffee, tea, chocolate, honey and bananas in supermarket chains. In the United Kingdom, Christian Aid launched a Global Supermarket Campaign urging supermarkets to establish a set of ethical principles for their purchases from the South and to implement an independently monitored code of conduct for all overseas suppliers of own-brand products by the year 2000.

Church-related organizations in Switzerland were successful in convincing the giant Migros supermarket chain to pressure Del Monte to ensure that conditions for pineapple plantation workers in the Philippines were improved. Since 1983, when Del Monte agreed, several monitoring visits have been paid to evaluate the implementation of the agreement.[2] Another Swiss campaign encourages buyers of athletic shoes to ask shops to adhere to a code of conduct guaranteeing workers who produce the shoes a decent salary, minimum social rights and freedom to organize.[3]

Working conditions in the textile and clothing industry are notoriously bad. While some seamstresses in Honduras may work 20 hours a day for 31 US cents an hour, conditions in the North are not always much better. In 1995 state officials in California freed 71 Thai immigrants from a sweatshop in Los Angeles. They had been forced to work for up to 17 hours a day, were held captive in a razor-wired compound and were paid between 60 cents and $1.60 an hour at a time when the legal minimum wage was $4.25. Encouraged by a survey showing that three-quarters of US shoppers would be willing to pay higher prices for clothing and shoes bearing a "No Sweat" label, it has been agreed to establish a code of conduct which prohibits child labour, forced labour and worker abuse, establishes health and safety standards, recognizes the right to join a union, limits working hours to 60 a week and insists that workers are paid at least the legal minimum wage in every country in which garments are made.

Child labour has become a growing international concern. According to the International Labour Office (ILO), in 1995 more than 30 percent of children in Bangladesh between 10 and 14 years were "economically active". While most of them work in the informal sector, many are employed in the clothing and textile industry, which is of great importance for the economy of Bangladesh. Between 1983 and 1995 the number of manufacturers of clothes in the country grew from 47 to 2224; and clothing exports rose from 4 to 63 percent of total exports. After the Child Labor Coalition in the USA threatened a boycott campaign, the clothing industry in Bangladesh signed an agreement with the ILO and UNICEF to end child labour in the production of clothes for export. Schools were established to rehabilitate the children, and it was agreed that parents of formerly employed children would receive a monthly compensation for income lost.

The International Confederation of Free Trade Unions (ICFTU) has signed an agreement with FIFA, the world football governing body, to ensure that footballs bearing its logo are not produced by using child labour. The code says that only workers over 15 will be employed, limits the work week to 48 hours, sets health and safety standards and acknowledges the rights of workers to form or join trade unions and bargain collectively.[4] Another international programme, Rugmark, has targeted the use of child labour in the production of hand-knotted carpets. Exporters may attach the Rugmark label to their carpets after meeting stringent requirements ensuring that no child labour is used and that official minimum wages are paid. Importers voluntarily contribute 1 percent of the export value of the carpets to support schools and vocational training for children.

Although the reduction of child labour can be applauded, these campaigns also leave some open questions. Since only about 5 percent of child workers are employed in export-oriented sectors, actions of this kind cannot finally solve the problem.[5] Only the reduction of absolute poverty can finally end child labour.

Moreover, Southern countries fear that new social and environmental regulations can be a disguised form of protectionism which increases their production costs, harms their competitiveness and thus reduces their access to Northern markets. Indeed, the US law on child labour stipulates that such labour should not endanger the jobs of adults in the North. Southern countries also argue that some of these trade measures are inherently unfair as they can only be used by the economically powerful against the weak. What comparable instrument might Bangladesh use to ensure that the North does not export products which have been produced with high carbon dioxide emissions?

Positive measures to encourage socially and environmentally responsible production, such as reduced taxes and lower tariffs, may be preferable to boycotts and bans. Rising consumer awareness of the social and environmental aspects of production can also provide new opportunities for Southern economies. Although only 6.5 percent of the OECD countries' consumption was met by imports from the South in 1996, this is expected to increase to 14 percent over the coming decade.[6] Many of the export products are in sectors where new social and environmental requirements are emerging. Innovative action is needed to link up with these newly emerging markets for fair trade products so that benefits can be reaped from the globalizing economy.

Growth rates in the fair trade sector often surpass those in other sectors. Producers of fair trade products receive higher prices for their products, can create more jobs and often benefit from more secure export outlets than their counterparts in conventional trade. The International Federation of Alternative Trade (IFAT), which groups the ATOs, has identified several differences between ATOs and conventional trade channels:

- They give priority to small producers who find it difficult to undertake export trade without a sympathetic marketing partner.
- They are specially interested in how producer groups are organized, preferring groups in which members have a say in running the organization and which provide such benefits as education and welfare schemes.
- They pay prices which allow the producer a reasonable return and often pay for orders in advance.
- They build their range around the products made by the producers they want to support.
- They promote their suppliers among their customers, giving information about the project, the locality and the difficulties faced by small producers.

– They aim to provide assistance with information on overseas marketing requirements and help with matters such as design, technology, packaging, labelling and sales promotion.[7]

Eco-wood

Tropical deforestation (an example is the Philippines, where 60 percent of the land was forested 40 years ago, compared to 10 percent today) is the object of intense scrutiny by Western environmentalists. This often annoys Southern governments, which accuse rich countries of hypocrisy (they razed their forests ages ago and produce 80 percent of the world's greenhouse gases) and protectionism. But the clearance of tropical forests is also a concern for local populations, which depend on them for their livelihood. The clash between the interests of local communities on the one hand and business and government on the other hand can result in violence. Frustrated local landowners on Pavuvu, in the Solomon Islands, set three bulldozers of a Malaysian logging firm on fire in 1995; a few months later an anti-logging leader was brutally killed.

In the Solomon Islands, uncontrolled logging – mostly by Malaysian and South Korean companies – continues at three times the estimated sustainable level, with forests predicted to be logged within the next ten to fifteen years. With logging accounting for 42 percent of exports, 16 percent of GDP and more than 60 percent of government revenues, forest depletion is a looming disaster for the Solomon Islands' economy. Meanwhile, local communities see their forests destroyed, their environment polluted and their land rights violated.

The United Church in the Solomon Islands is very much involved in efforts to improve the social situation in the country. In a review of its Integrated Human Development Programme in 1993, the church was asked to assist local communities in the marketing and transport of timber. The challenge was to find ways of combining environmentally sustainable timber production with a dependable income for the villagers. This led to the establishment of SWIFT – Solomon Western Islands Fair Trade – in 1994.

Under the supervision of foresters, forest management plans are developed in which small-scale and sustainable yields are the key elements. Full respect is paid to the land rights and the customary decision-making rules of the tribes and the local communities. To limit environmental destruction to a minimum, trees are sawn into beams and boards on the spot where they are felled and then carried from the forest. The timber is sold to a wholly owned Dutch subsidiary of SWIFT. SWIFT activities are based on the ten criteria for ecologically and socially sound forestry of the International Forest Stewardship Council (FSC), an independent non-profit organization.

Although the price for eco-wood is higher than that for "normal" tropical wood, SWIFT's supply can hardly keep up with demand. It now works with 300 village groups, covering 50,000 hectares of forest, and has generated US$750,000 for local producers. The price producers receive per tree is about 40 times higher than what is offered by the logging companies. SWIFT also offers an extensive package of courses on forestry, timber inspection, saw maintenance and bookkeeping. In addition, legal assistance is offered to groups which are disadvantaged by large woodcutting companies. SWIFT's non-profit activities are financed by ICCO, the Dutch inter-church organization for development cooperation.

LETS

A group in Montpelier, Vermont, has begun to print and circulate its own money to boost the local economy. Anyone can take part in this initiative by putting in US$5 in cash and receiving $40 in local bills called "Green Mountain Hours", which members agree to accept for goods and services. Since the scheme began in October 1996, more than 100 businesses have signed up.

This is one example of a growing number of initiatives by local communities to decrease their dependency on outside forces through an organized barter system. Since time immemorial people have exchanged goods and services without money. While the introduction of money has made economic systems much more efficient by eliminating the cumbersome task of finding a match for specific goods and services offered or asked, money economies can also create dependencies. Local Exchange Trading Systems (LETS) seek to reduce such dependencies.

The principle of LETS is very simple: points or local currency can be earned by offering goods and services to other members of the LETS, who pay an agreed number of accounting units. A central office keeps track of the members' balances, and no interest is charged on account balances. Since the accounting units can be spent only in the system in which they are issued, they do not have the same spending power as cash. They are not an alternative to cash but supplementary to it, and they reduce the dependency on normal money as well as on state benefits.

In a short period of time, LETS have become very popular in Canada, the USA, Australia and Great Britain. The largest system is based in Auckland, Aotearoa New Zealand, with more than 2000 members, including many small enterprises.

Unemployed self-help initiatives

Many unemployed persons would prefer organizing themselves and taking care of their own livelihoods to relying on handouts. In Aotearoa New Zealand, two People's Centres have been set up to organize the unemployed. The two centres have a membership of over 4000 families (some 12,000-13,000 individuals) which pay a fixed monthly membership fee of NZ$7 per family. With the proceeds, the People's Centres offer services like:
- completely free medical care;
- low-cost dental care;
- hairdressing for a price of NZ$2 (so that people can look better when they go for a job interview);
- free membership of the Green Dollar Exchanges (the LETS mentioned above);
- counselling, welfare advocacy, chaplaincy, budgeting, education and other similar personal services;
- cultural programmes which use music, art and drama as a method of building self-confidence and creativity, and

as a way to support the political work of the unemployed;
- training and support for people wanting to set up small businesses or cooperatives;
- research and publications on the causes of poverty and unemployment, both domestic and international;
- courses on people-centred development and community organizing.[8]

Mondragon

The Mondragon project in the Basque region of Spain was begun in 1941 when a Spanish priest, Don José Arizmendarreta, set up a school to teach methods of responsible agriculture. Shortly thereafter, he established a number of cooperatives. Mondragon today is an association of some 200 organizations, including 120 worker-owned, democratically controlled commercial enterprises. More than 22,000 workers, who are also the only owners of the organizations, have guaranteed jobs for life, fully adequate incomes, a broad health insurance plan for their families, a pension programme and an insurance programme which guarantees 80 percent of the latest salary received in case of unemployment.

Mondragon has its own bank, the Caja Laboral Popular, which defines money as an accounting and exchange tool, not a commodity. According to its unusual commercial loan policy, the riskier the loan, the lower the interest rate. Each cooperative shares in the ownership of the bank, which has rarely experienced a default on its uncollateralized loans. The cooperatives of Mondragon are more productive per person than any other group of workers in Spain, and their businesses are more than twice as profitable as the average conventional Spanish firm. When unemployment in the Basque region rose to 30 percent, Mondragon's employment was maintained.[9]

Micro-enterprises and micro-credit

Variously described as the informal sector, the underground economy or the black economy, the myriad activities taking place at the margin of the modern market economy provide an income for an increasing number of people in the South.

While the world's 500 largest corporations account for 25 percent of the global economic output, they employ only one-twentieth of one percent of the world's population. It is in much smaller enterprises that most people make their livelihoods. About half of the paid jobs in the world are held by people who work in one- to five-person enterprises, and in some places the percentage is even higher. According to the UN's *Human Development Report 1996*, the informal sector, in which many micro-enterprises are located, accounts for nearly 80 percent of all employment in Cotonou, Benin, and Ibadan, Nigeria, 68 percent in Bombay, India, and 66 percent in Douala, Cameroon. In Latin America and the Caribbean, more than 50 million micro-enterprises employ more than 150 million workers.

But the growth of micro-enterprises is not limited to the South. In the US, where bigger companies shed 645,000 jobs between 1992 and 1996, small and medium-sized businesses created 11.8 million new jobs.[10] In the North, the phenomenon often takes the form of an increasing number of consulting firms and independent contractors, as large companies shed jobs by implementing "leaner" production and organization models. In Eastern Europe, many have become hustlers, traders, independent manufacturers or free-lance dealmakers.

Micro-enterprises are not a panacea for human development in the South. They have a mixed record of successes and failures, and working conditions are often poor. Nevertheless, the potential of informal economies and the micro-enterprises that compose them should not be underestimated. Small businesses, with their high flexibility, absence of bureaucracy and speed of decision-making, may be better suited for many tasks than their larger counterparts. In many countries, the informal sector already has a higher growth rate than the formal sector, and in a more appropriate business and legal environment, micro-enterprises could become an even more dynamic sector than hitherto.

Micro-enterprises have several characteristics in common:
- *small scale*: people working in the informal sector often work alone or with unpaid family members;
- *labour intensity*: production is often manual, equipment simple and often hand-made, little division of labour;
- *minimal capital inputs*: investments range from a few dollars for the baskets and working capital of a street vendor, to a thousand dollars or more for the simple equipment and working capital of a shoemaker with five employees;
- *local market orientation*.[11]

The main constraint on micro-enterprises is their lack of access to productive assets, notably land and capital. To some extent, the situation has improved with the recent upsurge in micro-lending.

A decade ago micro-credit, the practice of lending small amounts of money, often without collateral, to poor would-be entrepreneurs, was on the fringes of international finance. Today, more than US$1 billion a year is being lent to some 8 million people in the South. Even the USA has about 300 micro-credit programmes.

Commercial banks are reluctant to extend loans to micro-enterprises. The costs of administering many small loans is considered too high, and micro-enterprises, which often cannot provide security or a collateral, are seen as a poor risk. Women are especially affected by local customs and even national laws which discriminate against them in economic life. The UN Development Programme says that in African countries where women make up more than 60 percent of the agricultural labour force and contribute up to 80 percent of total small-scale food production, they receive less than 10 percent of the credit to small farmers and only 1 percent of total credit to agriculture.

Unable to borrow from commercial banks, poor people often have to resort to money-lenders and loan sharks whenever they need emergency or small investment loans. The interest charged on such loans is usually very high. Those who cannot repay debts contracted in this way are forced to sell their small land-holdings, animals and even homes, eventually joining the ranks of the landless and the deprived.

However, over the last decade or so, pioneering micro-credit schemes across the South and in some parts of the North have shown that the poor are not a "bad risk", that they are prompt and reliable repayers (especially women) and that they successfully use small loans to increase their income. Leading micro-credit lenders around the world boast repayment rates of 97 percent and higher.

Micro-credit schemes come in many varieties. Some extend loans in local currencies, others in foreign currencies. Some provide grants for self-employment ventures, with repayment in community service; others provide farm animals as a "living loan" with offspring being considered as interest over the loan. Some schemes include a grant component to provide training in enterprise development, business management and market analysis. But all schemes have certain common characteristics. They are democratic and participatory, favour loans to groups or cooperatives rather than individuals, keep procedures for reviewing and approving loan applications simple and disburse small, short-term loans quickly. Because of their repayment record, women's groups are disproportionately highly represented among the receivers of micro-credit. Interest rates are kept as low as possible. Social and environmental criteria for loans are applied.

To promote micro-credit schemes all over the world, a summit was organized in February 1997 in Washington. Its declaration of intent spoke of a goal of 100 million poor entrepreneurs, 4 million in the North, having access to micro-credit by 2005. But the enthusiasm about micro-credit must be tempered by the recognition that while micro-credit is an efficient and successful additional instrument for human development, it is not sufficient. Micro-credit initiatives can achieve their full potential only if legal systems that discriminate against them and favour conventional lending are changed. Heavy foreign debt burdens, the rigour of structural adjustment programmes, agricultural policies of Northern (and Southern) countries and inequitable world trading systems constitute important hindrances to the success of micro-credit schemes.

Despite the impediments, micro-credit schemes flourish. Perhaps the best known is the Grameen Bank in Bangladesh. Landless people can obtain loans by joining a group of five borrowers who meet weekly with a bank officer trained to understand the needs of the poor. At first only two members of the group are allowed to apply for a loan. Depending on their performance in repayment, the next two can apply, and subsequently the fifth as well. The Grameen Bank now reaches one million rural clients, more than 90 percent of them women. The recovery rate of loans is 99 percent, something conventional banks can only dream of.[12]

Responsible investment

More and more individuals and institutions are applying social and environmental criteria in addition to financial considerations when they take investment decisions.[13] Since the beginning of the 1980s, the value of investments guided by other than financial motives has risen from US$40 billion to $650 billion.[14] US religious organizations have invested more than $300 million in community economic development with the help of the Interfaith Center on Corporate Responsibility (ICCR) in New York. Many religious organizations have drawn up social responsibility guidelines for their investments. While there are differences of opinion about what makes for "responsible" or "ethical" investment, most use three strategies:

- *avoidance* or *disinvestment*: not placing money in companies which produce (for example) arms, alcohol or tobacco, which apply discriminatory employment policies, which support violations of human rights, are involved in nuclear energy or contribute substantially to environmental destruction;
- *advocacy*: using investments as leverage to promote corporate responsibility through shareholders resolutions and/or negotiations with management;

– *alternative investment*: a deliberate choice to invest in enterprises deemed to behave in a socially and environmentally responsible way.

Investments guided by social and environmental criteria have proved to give a financial yield equal to or better than that of "normal" investments. For example, from 1985 to 1993, the Friends Provident Stewardship pension fund in the United Kingdom provided an annualized return of 20.2 percent. In 1993, it returned 31.3 percent. In the same year, the Friends Provident Stewardship income fund – also ethically managed – returned 41.3 percent.[15]

EDCS

In the 1970s, the ecumenical movement was actively engaged in opposing foreign investments in South Africa and bank loans to the apartheid regime. Many South African blacks and some others had pleaded with the international community to cut foreign economic ties with their country in support of their anti-apartheid struggle. Some who supported these campaigns suggested that their credibility would be enhanced if alternative ways of investment were also established.

At the same time, a discussion was going on in the ecumenical movement about the advantages and disadvantages of grants and loans for development. Traditionally, churches and church-related organizations in the North have participated in efforts to promote human development by making available grants and personnel. The churches' own investments were managed to yield a maximum financial return in order to safeguard the financial future of the churches and their programmes. Awareness grew that investment money should at least in part be used to support the message and the ministry of the churches. In the South, more and more people were discovering that working with loans rather than grants preserved their dignity and promoted greater self-reliance. And once repaid, the money lent could be "recycled" – used to the advantage of poor people elsewhere.

These considerations led the WCC in the early 1970s to establish the Ecumenical Development Co-operative Society (EDCS). EDCS lends to commercially viable enterprises that comply with a set of social and environmental criteria. Its capital originates with churches and church-related organizations, which can become shareholders of EDCS. Individuals can buy certificates of shares through support organizations. Each shareholder has one vote in the shareholders' meeting, independent of the number of shares held. Thus, a church in the South with only a few shares cannot be outvoted by a rich church in the North which can afford to buy many shares.

Shareholders in EDCS usually receive an annual dividend of 2 percent – lower than the financial return on "normal" investments, but the social return is higher. By accepting a relatively low financial return, churches, church-related organizations and others are thus challenged to demonstrate that living out Christian faith in economic life is more than going after the highest possible financial return. It has been estimated that EDCS has been instrumental over the years in creating and safeguarding some 12,000 jobs on all continents. In 1995, the WCC decided that by the year 2000, 10 percent of its investments should be in the EDCS.

Much earlier, the Ecumenical Church Loan Fund (ECLOF) was set up to help rebuild church buildings destroyed during the second world war. Subsequently, ECLOF has provided low-interest loans to small business enterprises in the South through national revolving funds. With instruments like grants, ECLOF and EDCS, the ecumenical movement now has available a broad spectrum of complementary instruments to stimulate human development and economic alternatives aimed at promoting justice, peace and respect for creation through the use of money.

Loans for development cannot always replace grants. For example, activities which generate little or no income will always have to rely on grants. But for other types of activities, loans are becoming increasingly important, especially in view of the stagnation or decline in official development assistance and the deteriorating financial situation of churches in the North. Having achieved a certain degree of ecclesiastical independence, churches in the South are now shifting their attention to financial independence through setting up income-generating activities – often financed with loans – in an effort to become truly local churches.[16]

* * *

Our concern for a just household – a just economy – requires that we discern the signs of the times (Matt. 16:3). In the preceding chapters we have sought to do that. The signs of the times concerning the use of the three traditional production factors in the household – labour, capital and land – produce an ambivalent picture. Great advances have been made, but we can also hear creation groaning and many people crying. The knowledge brought by science and technology – in a sense a fourth production factor – and economic growth have improved the quality of life for many people. Their work is much less drudgery than that of their grandparents was. Their health is improving, they live longer lives, and they often enjoy more time for leisure. Improved education has decreased ignorance tremendously, and communication technologies and transportation systems have made it increasingly difficult to suppress freedom of expression and opinion. The hopeful examples given in this last chapter are also important signs of the times.

Yet our global household is also the scene of large-scale destruction of the natural environment and growing polarization between rich and poor. In his 1987 encyclical letter *Sollicitudo Rei Socialis*, Pope John Paul II warned that "superdevelopment" can easily make people slaves of possessions. The pope spoke about "blind submission to pure consumerism", "crass materialism", the "cult of having", the "flood of publicity and ceaseless and tempting offers of products", and the "all-consuming desire for profit" – all constituting a "temptation to idolatry" (paras 28-30). Large-scale unemployment deprives millions of people of a sense of purpose in life. Communities are undermined and social relationships are under great pressure and even broken. New forms of alienation are creating apathy, resignation, cynicism, drug addiction, senseless violence and despair.

The signs of the times are thus ambiguous. Science and technology have a liberating effect, but the very forces of progress can also spell disaster (nuclear and biological weapons), or take on a dynamic of their own which seems difficult to control when they become masters rather than servants. Developments in the field of genetic engineering may even make us feel like God.

It is not easy to live out the Christian faith in times such as these. Although, with some notable exceptions, Christians are not being systematically persecuted for their faith today, many feel subject to organized as well as hidden temptations which can be experienced as forms of persecution (think of aggressive advertising and the struggle to "keep up with the Joneses"). In economic life, "thou *shalt* covet" seems to have become the law of the land. Martin Luther's application of the commandment "thou shalt not steal" to economic life seems to have been forgotten, as is the case with the commandments concerning idolatry and misusing the name of God.

The integrity of the Christian faith is threatened by the pantheon of false gods which surround us, demanding our worship and our sacrifices. Nobody is immune to these idols; if we have a chance, all of us venture a little dance around the golden calf from time to time.

If idolatry is indeed an issue, as Pope John Paul II discerns, a major task is to "secularize" economic life and to exorcise the false gods. In this sense, economic life is a vast mission field for the churches. But churches and Christians are objects as well as subjects of this mission, because we are part and parcel of the existing system and the prevailing ideology. The mission task to demask false gods is awesome; the Old Testament story of the destruction of the golden calf speaks of its being accompanied by the killing of 3000 people. However, there is no time to give way to fear and despair. The belief in powerlessness is always self-fulfilling.